This Book Belongs To
Michael F. Killeen

Enhancing Teaching

Enhancing Teaching

Madeline Hunter
University of California at Los Angeles

Macmillan College Publishing Company
New York
Maxwell Macmillan Canada
Toronto
Maxwell Macmillan International
New York Oxford Singapore Sydney

Cover art: Marsha McDivett
Editor: Debra A. Stollenwerk
Production Editor: Mary Irvin
Art Coordinator: Lorraine Woost
Photo Editor: Anne Vega
Cover Designer: Russ Maselli
Production Buyer: Jeff Smith
Electronic Text Management: Ben Ko, Marilyn Wilson Phelps
Illustrations: Jane Lopez

This book was set in Dutch 823 by Macmillan College Publishing Company
and was printed and bound by Book Press, Inc., a Quebecor America Book
Group Company. The cover was printed by New England Book Components.

Macmillan College Publishing Company
866 Third Avenue
New York, NY 10022

Macmillan College Publishing Company is part of the
Maxwell Communication Group of Companies.

Maxwell Macmillan Canada, Inc.
1200 Eglinton Avenue East, Suite 200
Don Mills, Ontario M3C 3N1

Library of Congress Cataloging-in-Publication Data
Hunter, Madeline C.
    Enhancing teaching / Madeline Hunter.
      p.   cm.
    Includes bibliographical references and index.
    ISBN 0-02-358941-8
      1. Teaching. 2. Decision-making. 3. Education—Curricula.
  4. Learning. Psychology of. I. Title.
    LB1025.3.H85   1994
    371.1'02—dc20   93-18792
                                           CIP

Printing: 1 2 3 4 5 6 7 8 9   Year: 4 5 6 7

Photo credits: Supplied by author: pp.7, 11, 14, 22, 25, 26, 32, 34, 44, 60, 61,
69, 72, 81, 83, 89, 109, 120 ,126, 132, 136, 142, 145, 160, 174, 199, 204, 210,
217, 224, 234, 242, 244; Anne Vega/Macmillan: pp. 8, 21, 31, 43, 53, 66, 107,
119, 135, 141, 156, 165, 209, 214, 243; Barbara Schwartz/Macmillan: pp. 79,
93, 168; Sunrise/Trinity: p. 222; KS Studios/Macmillan: p. 232.

A creative teacher is one who has first acquired the necessary skills to practice the science of instruction and who continues to refine and supplement those skills in such a way as to capitalize on his/her own personal strengths, those unique qualities of the learners, and the individual features of the teaching/learning environment in which students and teachers find themselves.

—Author unknown

Preface

I began my professional career as a clinical psychologist at the Los Angeles Children's Hospital. It was a depressing job. One is not eager to get up in the morning when the first task of the day is to prepare parents for their child's nonrecovery. So I moved to Los Angeles Juvenile Hall, which wasn't much better, but at least these youngsters' problems were potentially curable. I found that in many cases the problem could have been prevented, but I could deliver only too little too late. So I became a school psychologist to work on prevention rather than remediation.

It was then that I learned that every teacher and administrator had taken a course in Educational Psychology. In it, they had learned about slobbering dogs and pecking pigeons, about Freud, Rogers, Piaget, and Maslow, but none of it taught in a way that could inform future decision making in a classroom.

Consequently, I began translating research-based psychological generalizations into teacher language, so they could be used in planning learning opportunities, implementing those plans, and evaluating the results before replanning. Teachers were grateful to have their procedures articulated as psychological principles that validated what they previously had been doing on only an intuitive basis using their creativity and artistry; if they were not successful, they welcomed suggestions for more effective procedures.

Since then, I have tried to keep abreast of the research in psychology, education, sociology, and neurology—an impossible task! But I have translated what I consider to be their most relevant findings from research jargon into ideas for "what to do tomorrow morning with these kids and this content."

So much new is known about cause and probable effects (nothing is certain with the human) of a teacher's decisions and actions that I would be violating the very principles I preach if I tried to "cover" it in one book. This book and my many others endeavor to make pertinent research available to teachers, with examples relevant to their daily decisions and actions.

The book will be useful to instructors and students in teacher education courses and will help build a sound base for subsequent educational decisions. Current education students are fortunate: they don't have to learn so much by trial and error; they are inheriting the legacy of articulated knowledge that wasn't available in past years. (The writer feels she should look up her first year's salary and return it, because clearly it was embezzled—although the work was the result of the best she knew at the time.)

This book also will be useful to the teachers and administrators in the field. It will remind them of the powerful impact of professional decisions on student learning and that these decisions should be made intentionally from a knowledge base. It also will enable those who are responsible for coaching teachers to recognize, articulate, and appreciate effectiveness when they observe professional decisions skillfully implemented.

To my own teachers from kindergarten to the current educational giants who are producing research, I owe a great debt of gratitude. I am one of those fortunate students who has been stimulated by my own family and by researchers, colleagues, and students in psychology and education. They all continue to inspire, teach, goad, and perplex me into becoming a "learnaholic." It's a wonderful affliction!

I also express my appreciation to Deb Stollenwerk, editor; Mary Irvin, production editor; Lorry Woost, art coordinator; Anne Vega, photo editor; Russs Maselli, cover designer; and Jane Lopez, artist, at Macmillan who brought this book into being.

About the Book

Great teachers have existed since the beginning of time. Frequently, their teaching was intuitive, not a conscious and deliberate use of research-based behaviors that would predictably increase learning. There is no question that there exists an art of teaching over and beyond effective teaching. In the last half of this century, however, we have learned that there also is a science that underlies and enhances the art. Science can be used to accelerate, and make more predictable, students' successful accomplishment. Science also builds a launching pad from which the art of the teacher can ascend to new heights.

This book was written in response to requests for gathering together, in a single book, many journal articles, as well as presentations and workshop handouts that teachers have found useful. *It is not meant to be all inclusive.* Much of the science of instruction (pedagogy) has been developed in depth in my other books, many of which focused on helping teachers implement specific principles of learning. This book includes professional information and practical techniques based on implementation of a combination of many scientific principles. Those principles and techniques are useful to every teacher regardless of the teaching model being used or the organization of the learning environment. The reader will detect redundancies in different sections and chapters in the book: basic principles of learning reoccur as they apply to different topics, content, and situations.

For those who wish to examine the research basis from which these techniques are derived, it can be found in any educational psychology text. Short bibliographies of useful sources are provided at the end of the chapters.

The first section of this book, A Model of Teaching, describes the genesis of a decision-making model of teaching, based on principles derived from my study of psychology and related fields, plus observation and analysis of outstanding teachers. It is *a* model, not *the* model. It simply provides an organizational basis for planning, implementing, analyzing, and describing teaching. It is concerned with the "anatomy and physiology" of teaching in terms of the daily decisions every teacher makes consciously, intuitively, or by default. This section also addresses the misinformation that often accompanies discussion or evaluation of the decision-making model.

The second section, Decisions About Content, is focused on the decisions that every teacher must make regardless of the particular content or of the age, ability, or ethnicity of the students being taught. We do not deny variance but emphasize much of the invariance of human learning. The focus of this book is primarily on the *how* of assisting students to attain any learning, rather than on determining the learning that is worth being attained. The chapter on concepts, generalizations, and discriminations, however, does emphasize the value and transfer potential of teaching these general concepts, which are essential to higher-level thinking. We limit students by teaching only specifics.

The content section concludes with the elements to be considered in designing instruction, regardless of the model of teaching or delivery system to the student. This chapter covers the most misunderstood and misrepresented, but most popular and widely used, aspect of our work—the elements to be considered in lesson design. Unfortunately, the elements are sometimes interpreted as a "must do" edict rather than "must know about and think about." The elements were intended to be considered by the teacher to decide what might be best to do with particular students working with particular content in a particular situation.

The third section, Decisions About Learning Behaviors, is directed to the findings of contemporary research on the operation of the brain and the differences in students' learning preferences. These areas have come into prominence during the research of the last decade. The section begins with a brief review of what is now known about how the brain functions, as well as how a teacher can use that knowledge to help students develop proficiency in learning. Rather than spending time testing for or discovering a learner's preferred modality, which may change from task to task, the reader is advised to become proficient with many modality input systems and use them all. Instead of costly, one-to-one tutoring or individually created assignments, which were an early interpretation of "individualizing instruction," suggestions for ways to "individualize in the group" make the necessary "custom tailoring" possible for a teacher with a full class load and no assistants.

The final section of the book, Decisions About Teaching Behaviors, addresses diverse concerns expressed by teachers in the field. The section contains many suggestions for ways to increase learning without an increase of instruction time: getting the greatest learning dividends for time invested; exploring ways to increase students' understandings and active involvement in learning and generating meaning for themselves; using examples effectively; helping students acquire and internalize basic skills more effectively in all content areas so that students can accomplish higher-level tasks more efficiently.

The concluding chapters raise questions about some traditional practices in every classroom and suggest productive changes in formerly accepted teaching behaviors, such as repeating students' answers and current assessment practices.

It is the wish of the author that this book will make an additional contribution to the knowledge base for the decisions all teachers make, and to affirm the belief that teachers are decision-making professionals whose knowledge must continually be extended.

Students will be the beneficiaries of these goals by achieving more successful and satisfying learning. Teachers will be the beneficiaries by increasing their success and satisfaction in the profession of education. Society will be the beneficiary by the production of a better world in which to live.

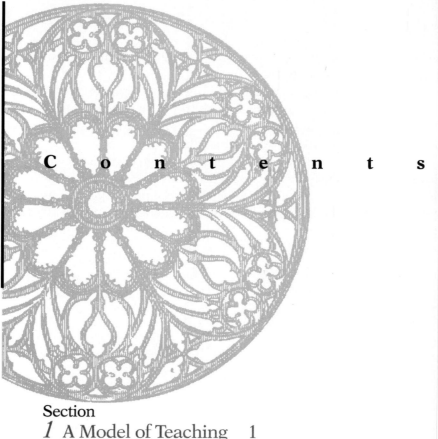

Contents

S e c t i o n

1

A Model of Teaching

Back in the "good old days" (which weren't very good—the author was around then!), there was little science in the preparation or ongoing development of skilled teachers. "Teachers are born, not made" was the erroneous assumption of many people. There existed avowed techniques ("Don't smile until Christmas"), but there was little research-based evidence for those teaching techniques that seemed effective and no organized pedagogical theory from which professional practice could be derived.

As a result, many teachers taught as they had been taught, or, through observational learning, they imitated current teachers, without knowing or being able to articulate why they were

1

using some techniques and not using others. Researchers in education had little contact with teachers in the field, and practitioners were only dimly aware of the implications of research for their daily practice.

We were beginning to address these concerns at the University of California at Los Angeles when along came *Sputnik* and the space race with the Soviet Union began. As a result, the focus of the nation was on schools, and our inquiry and research into the question "How do you become a skilled teacher?" became a center of attention and was recognized as important. The general design and results of our work on this fundamental question are discussed in this first section of the book.

Our work resulted in a model of teaching that we call the teacher decision-making model. This model (1) emerged from examination of research and from informed observations of successful teaching; (2) incorporates psychological principles, as well as current cognitive research into the functioning of the brain; (3) and provides an organization scheme for planning, implementing, and analyzing decisions that affect both teaching and learning.

In the creation of the model, observations of many styles of successful teaching—from preschool through high school and university, performed for a variety of content areas and through a variety of organizational patterns—had to be translated into practical teaching suggestions for the classroom. In addition, the teaching suggestions had to be a valid extrapolation from current research.

The teacher decision-making model is centered on the *teacher*, who, utilizing research, experience, and intuition, makes and implements decisions in three categories, in cooperation with students: content (what is to be learned), learning behaviors (what students will do to learn), and teaching behaviors (how teachers use the principles of learning to increase the probability of successful outcomes).

The three categories are discussed generally in this first section of the book. (Each of the remaining three major sections of the book focuses on one of the categories.) In addition, this first section gives a general description of the principles and history behind the teacher decision-making model.

The analysis of psychological principles, our work with helping teachers plan successful lessons, and a study of curriculum—all combined to lead to our identifying basic elements that must be considered in the design of effective lessons. These elements are (1) anticipatory set, which develops readiness to learn; (2) the instructional objective and its value to the learners; (3) the source and type of instructional input; (4) a model or example of the intended learning outcome; (5) a check for learners' understanding of the objective; (6) guided/monitored practice; and (7) independent practice to help learners develop fluency and retain what has been learned. (See chapter 8 for a more detailed discussion of these elements.) The teacher's role in deciding which elements to include or exclude for a particular lesson is the key to successful achievement by students.

Unfortunately, some people, in their zeal to reduce the complexity of the teaching process, have misinterpreted our model for designing lessons by viewing it as a rigid system of "steps" that must be included in every learning situation. This was never the intent of our model. The actual intent and nature of the model will unfold through reading of the chapters in this first section.

Chapter 1 describes the genesis of a teacher decision-making model that, for the first time, effected a synthesis of relevant research and a method for using that research in daily teaching decisions. Those decisions must be made regardless of the content being learned, the teaching model being used, or the age, ability, or ethnicity of the learners. There is nothing that a teacher must always do except *think* and teach in a way that maintains the dignity of every learner. There are implications from research that every teacher should deliberately consider before making and implementing professional decisions.

Chapter 2 traces the development of the relatively new science of psychology and its contributions to educational research, as well as to the professional development of educators. Described are the contributions of behavioral research, which gave the new science of psychology its credibility, and those of cognitive research, which gave psychology its substance.

Chapter 3 addresses misconceptions that arose as a result of attributing "should do" to research results that needed to be "known and considered" by practicing educators, but that were not mandates. In their well-intentioned aspiration to incorporate research in daily practice, legislators, boards, and administrators mandated practices such as using checklists to validate "presence or absence" of techniques when they should have been using that research themselves to determine appropriateness of teachers' decisions in terms of student outcomes and the professional artistry and creativity with which teachers were implementing decisions.

Finally, chapter 4 raises questions regarding the use and abuse of our teacher decision-making model, emphasizing the model's aim of establishing professional principles and structure, rather than imposing constraints.

The ultimate purpose of the section is to introduce the reader to a model of teaching that weaves the "patchwork" of the different focuses of research into a "professional tapestry" to be known, understood, appreciated, and used by every educational practitioner in the real world of students.

1

The Origin of a Teacher Decision-Making Model

A creative teacher is one who has acquired the skills necessary to practice the science of instruction and who continues to refine and supplement those skills in such a way as to capitalize on his/her own personal strengths, those unique qualities of the learners, and the individual features of the teaching/learning environment in which students and teachers find themselves.

Author Unknown

Do teachers make a difference? The research-based answer to that question is an unequivocal "Yes!" What is it about teachers that makes the difference? Here the answer is not so clear, but studies have shown that it is not what a teacher is, or how a teacher feels, but how a teacher *thinks*—which results in what a teacher *does*—that has potential for affecting and effecting students' achievement.

Teaching can be defined as the process of making and implementing decisions before, during, and after instruction—decisions that, when implemented, increase the probability of learning. If what a teacher does is artistic (that is, shows creativity and sensitivity to the situation) and is consistent with what is now known about cause-effect relationships in learning, and if the teacher's decisions and actions reflect awareness of the current state of the learner and the present environment, then the probability of students' learning should predictably increase.

These qualities of professional decision making are a far cry from the "dedicated and loves kids" product of many former teacher education programs. Now, adequate professional teacher preparation parallels that of other professions like medicine. It requires the professional to learn, internalize, and implement with *artistry* the contributions of science plus one's own intuition to increase productive functioning. For the teaching professional, the scientific principles must always be interpreted in light of the needs of the learner in his/her particular life space and be modified to accommodate those needs.

Let's look at a common example of the interaction of *science and situation* in decision making in teaching. Johnny is studying division of fractions and is just catching on to "invert the divisor and multiply." Research suggests that repeated (massed) practice (going over it several times) at this initial stage of understanding results in faster and more durable learning. Therefore, Johnny should do two or three more problems that are relevant to his own life and experience before he leaves for recess. However, Johnny's team has a baseball game organized for recess and if he's afraid he'll be late for the game, he won't have his mind on what he's doing. His feelings of discomfort can become associated with fractions in particular and math in general. What to do? Would it be a wise idea to keep him for a couple of minutes to cement his understanding? Or would it be better to let him go today and have him be unsure in math tomorrow while his classmates are confident? There is no predetermined correct answer. The teacher must make a decision on his/her feet, including the option of letting Johnny decide. (Researchers have time to make such considered decisions on their seats!)

This synthesis of science and sensitivity to a situation explains why we can't supply pat answers to teachers. We can, however, equip educators with research-validated principles on which to base their deci-

The same categories of teaching decisions need to be addressed regardless of whether students are working individually, in cooperative groups, or in large groups.

sions while adapting them to the individuality of students and situations. Adequate professional preparation requires all the following:

1. Basic instruction in cause-effect principles of teaching, learning, and curriculum

2. Observation of expert teaching, followed by *guided* practice *during* teaching in responding to cues emitted by students in many different situations

3. Study of the curricular areas for which that teacher is responsible

4. Planning, with guidance, of specific lessons before teaching

5. Teaching the lessons with coaching and/or reflective analysis of the results

While we were designing a program that would produce a professional teacher capable of effective, high-speed decision making, it was decided that it was necessary for us as teacher educators working at UCLA to equip the aspiring teacher with content expertise and then to translate four components into action:

1. Factor analysis of the stream of decisions made in teaching so that necessary cause-effect relationships could be identified and appropriate behaviors selected
2. Preservice instruction designed to *teach and model* those cause-effect relationships in the transmission of professional infor-

Teachers in groups or in staff meetings continually examine their practice and learn new skills to enhance their teaching.

mation and skills to beginning teachers (they need to see us practice what we preach)

3. Production of filmed and videotaped episodes demonstrating effective teaching in each category of decisions, so that prescribed instructional sequences would utilize the principles of modeling and observational learning

4. Development of a diagnostic, prescriptive observation instrument that would identify and label effective performance or action pattern skills used by the teacher (not what the teacher intended but what s/he did), as well as identifying those skills that still needed to be refined or learned

In this chapter, it will be possible to give only a brief description of each of these four components. (They are described in detail in many of my other works, which are listed in the bibliography at the end of this chapter. Note the videotapes listed there are ones produced for professional teacher development.)

Analysis of Decisions Made in Any Teaching Model

All teaching decisions cluster into three categories: content, learning behaviors, and teaching behaviors.

Content to Be Learned

While state mandates, curriculum guides, district policy, and textbooks may identify the general goals and content of instruction, the teacher must determine the appropriate level of difficulty for each day's learning opportunity and must ascertain when students are ready to proceed to the next, more difficult learning. It is important to emphasize that such day-to-day decisions do not require elaborate and time-consuming diagnostic instruments, but rather an understanding of the incremental nature of most learning.

In some learning, teacher and student have no choice of sequence, because each learning is dependent on achievement of certain prior learnings. (Students can't multiply and divide if they don't understand addition and subtraction. Students can't think analytically when they have no information or don't understand the information.)

In other sequences, learnings are independent of each other and can be acquired in any order. (A student can learn to incorporate descriptive words in his or her writing before or after learning topic sentences. A student can learn metric measurement before or after learning feet and inches.) In an independent sequence, teacher and learner may choose the order of learning on the basis of interest, availability of materials, or convenience.

To make successful content decisions, the teacher must be able to discriminate between dependent and independent learning sequences, to break a complex learning task down into its simpler components (the process called task analysis), and to diagnose students in terms of those components that have already been learned and those that remain to be acquired.

To focus teacher and pupil energy and effort at the place where a student's knowledge or skill leaves off and new learning needs to begin, the teacher, *while* teaching, must utilize continuing informal diagnosis and make decisions as to whether to reteach, strengthen the learning with further practice, proceed to the next learning, or end the lesson because "now's not the time."

> One of the most pernicious problems in teaching is the teacher's desire to "cover material." Many teachers feel that they do not have time to discover and remedy their pupil's lack of information or skill because they would never be able to "cover" the material called for in the course; so they plunge ahead from a starting point that many of their students have never reached, and they proceed to teach the unknown by the incomprehensible. The result is that the student does not learn effectively and ends the course about where he started.
>
> *Pressley*

Astute planning and "on your feet" decisions pay tremendous dividends in increased student learning in relation to the time expended, as well as in the resulting satisfaction on the part of both student and teacher.

After instruction, the teacher uses objective evidence of the effectiveness of instruction to build correction into subsequent content decisions. For example, classroom performance indicates that the majority of students still need practice with their number facts, but they are getting bored. Should they be given a respite and work on some math that is not dependent on calculation, or should a novel way of practicing be introduced to rekindle their interest and effort? Clearly, the most eminent learning theorist, removed from the situation, could not make this decision. Only the teacher on site has the information necessary to make a decision with a high probability of satisfying consequences. (For the same reason, control was moved from the NASA scientists with their computers to the astronauts in the space capsule, who had "on site" feelings and perceptions from information that was so subtle it was not recorded in the computers on the ground.)

Learning Behaviors

Research has begun to formalize what teachers always knew intuitively: that students learn in different ways. Teaching decisions in this category do not require formal diagnosis of students to identify the preferred learning modality of each. Teaching decisions should be based on the

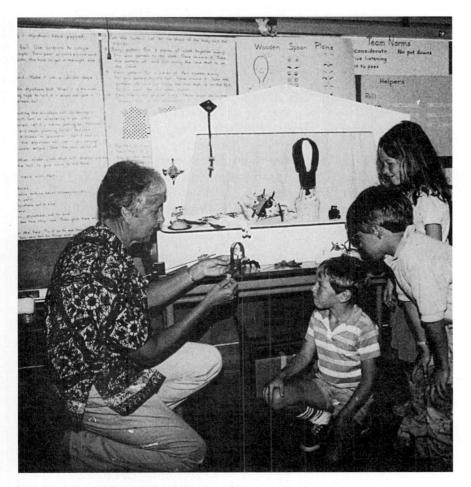

Students' observational learning behaviors, plus the teacher's questions, guide learning without supplying answers.

appropriateness of the learning behavior in relation to the content and on the need for encouraging students' practice in many modalities so that they develop a repertoire of learning styles.

In examining what students might do to achieve the desired learning, a teacher needs to consider building effective combinations of input behaviors into the instructional plan. For example, students might "see and say," "diagram and describe," "hear and indicate," "write and examine," "work alone or with others." At other times, the teacher deliberately limits students to the use of one input modality for purposes of diagnosing student use of the modality and/or strengthening that modality.

As a result of informal, inferential diagnosis *while teaching*, the teacher must decide when it is necessary to change or augment input. (S/he might add modeling, diagraming, having each student do, observe, verbally direct, choose, select.) The success of a "multi" or "uni" modality approach must be validated by an affirmative answer to the question "Is there perceivable evidence that students are achieving?" If the answer is no, the teacher needs to make modifications during instruction. (Another "on your feet" decision!)

Different models of teaching reflect the source of the input. In cooperative learning, information comes from the group. In discovery, input comes from observation, hypothesizing, and validating. In computer-assisted instruction, information comes from the computer. The source of input is the only way that models of teaching differ. The same three categories of decisions—about content, learning behaviors, and teaching behaviors—made by teacher or student, occur in every model of teaching.

During all instruction, regardless of the model, the teacher should elicit objective evidence of students' understanding. This constitutes a change from "I hope they learned" to "I know they learned because they demonstrated that learning by ____." If student understanding is not evident, the teacher needs to design additional learning opportunities in order to encourage students' achievement and then validate it. The determination must be made *while teaching* as to whether additional practice, remediation, or the next learning should occur now or be planned for a subsequent learning opportunity.

Teaching Behaviors

The primary responsibility of every professional is to render the service needed by the client, not what the professional prefers. Therefore, teaching behaviors are determined by student need, not teacher style. Skilled teachers have a repertoire of styles. *Before* instruction, a teacher should anticipate the student and teacher behaviors that would best facilitate learning. *During* instruction, those behaviors should be modified if they are perceived as being ineffective. For example, during teaching, a teacher needs to determine whether a particular student should be immediately accountable or be given additional time before having to demonstrate achievement. Should a student proceed to the next learning after one demonstration of competence, or are several validations required for that particular student to retain what has been learned? Should the teacher, at this moment, be supportive or demanding? Questions such as these can be answered only with information emerging from the immediate situation. Answers are always based on validated principles that affect learning, but they are modified as necessary for individual students in particular situations.

Staff Development: A Time to Model Effective Teaching

When teachers experience professional development that models effective instructional decision making, they more predictably learn to make and implement decisions with artistry. Preservice and inservice training capable of providing such models is very different from traditional teacher education and staff development, which often violated the very principles they were designed to teach.

Films and videotapes plus "live teaching" make it possible for new and experienced teachers to see professional decision making implemented at high speed in a typical classroom. Such observation facilitates learning the process of educational decision making and capitalizes on the power of observational learning. Research into the processing by the brain has validated the learning gain that results from integrating right and left hemispheric processing, that is, using both seeing and hearing, pictures and words. Therefore, "showing what we mean" is one powerful way of "practicing what we preach."

Analysis of Teaching: A Tool to Enhance Professional Effectiveness

Effective teaching requires performing a task analysis of a complex learning and then a diagnosis to identify which components a student has achieved and which remain to be accomplished. In the same way, performing an analysis of the complex process of successful teaching has resulted in diagnostic-prescriptive supervision and coaching to achieve the goal of continually enhancing teaching. The *trained* observer can

An informed observer's growth-evoking feedback is essential to continuing growth in teaching excellence.

identify teaching behaviors that research *plus classroom evidence* would support as increasing the probability of learning. Bringing these behaviors to the conscious awareness of every teacher and articulating why they are effective increases the likelihood that the teacher will make deliberate and appropriate use of those principles in the future. Teacher behaviors that use up time and energy but contribute nothing to students' learning also can be identified and eliminated. Informed observation productively reveals teaching decisions and actions that, albeit unintentionally, interfere with or slow students' successful accomplishment. Solving the mystery of "what went wrong" can suggest successful remediation for incorrect student responses.

Conclusion

All four components described in this chapter are necessary to professional development: (1) identification of the decisions a teacher must make; (2) staff development that enables the teacher to combine science and art in teaching; (3) films, tapes, and "live teaching" that provide opportunities for the teacher to see how it looks in the classroom; and (4) diagnostic-prescriptive coaching that provides reflective, growth-evoking feedback on professional performance. All of these components are now being used successfully in preservice as well as inservice professional education all over the world.

These components, which form the basis of effective teaching decisions and actions, are not the only answer to enhanced teaching. However, they constitute one avenue to professional competence that has been demonstrated not only to enhance students' learning but also to increase teachers' sense of professionalism through knowing what they're doing, doing it on purpose, and finding that it makes a measurable difference in their own and students' satisfaction and achievement.

Bibliography

The following materials are all by the author and further develop the concepts and principles of translating psychological principles into classroom practice. (Note that materials published by TIP Publications are available by writing to TIP Publications, P.O. Box 415, El Segundo, CA 90045.)

Books

Hunter, M. (1967). *Motivation theory for teachers*. El Segundo, CA: TIP Publications.

Hunter, M. (1967). *Retention theory for teachers*. El Segundo, CA: TIP Publications.

Hunter, M. (1969). *Teach more—faster*. El Segundo, CA: TIP Publications.

Hunter, M. (1971). *Teach for transfer*. El Segundo, CA: TIP Publications.

Hunter, M. (1976). *Prescription for improved instruction*. El Segundo, CA: TIP Publications.

Hunter, M. (1983). *Mastery teaching*. El Segundo, CA: TIP Publications.

Hunter, M. (1989). *Mastering coaching and supervision*. El Segundo, CA: TIP Publications.

Hunter, M. (1990). *Discipline that develops self-discipline*. El Segundo, CA: TIP Publications.

Hunter, M. (1992). *How to change to a nongraded school*. Alexandria, VA: Association for Supervision and Curriculum Development.

Hunter, M., & Breit, S. (1976). *Aide-ing in education*. El Segundo, CA: TIP Publications.

Hunter, M., & Carlson, P. V. (1977). *Improving your child's behavior*. El Segundo, CA: TIP Publications.

Hunter, M., & Lawrence, G. (1978). *Parent-teacher conferencing*. El Segundo, CA: TIP Publications.

Chapters in Books

Hunter, M. (1979). Individualization of foreign language learning. In M. Brown & M. H. Hunter (Eds.), *Foreign language learning, today and tomorrow: Essays in honor of E. M. Birkmaier.* New York: Pergamon.

Hunter, M. (1981). The impact of the essentials education approach to teachers and teaching. In *Essentials approach: Rethinking the curriculum for the 80s.* Washington, DC: U.S. Department of Educational Basic Skills Improvement Program.

Hunter, M. (1984). Knowing, teaching, and supervising. In P. L. Hosford (Ed.), *Using what we know about teaching* (pp. 169–192). Alexandria, VA: Association for Supervision and Curriculum Development.

Hunter, M. (1985). Standards in elementary education. In W. J. Johnston (Ed.), *Education on trial: Strategies for the future.* San Francisco, CA: Institute for Contemporary Studies.

Hunter, M. (1988). Create rather than await your fate in teacher evaluation. In S. Stanley & J. Popham (Eds.), *Teacher evaluation: Six prescriptions for success.* Alexandria, VA: Association for Supervision and Curriculum Development.

Hunter, M. (1990). Thoughts on staff development. In B. Joyce (Ed.), *Changing school culture through staff development.* Alexandria, VA: Association for Supervision and Curriculum Development.

Videotapes for Staff Development

Tapes with preschool through grade seven students. Aptos: CA: Special Purpose Films. (A descriptive brochure can be obtained by writing Special Purpose Films, 416 Rio del Mar, Aptos, CA 95003, or calling (408) 688-6320.)

Tapes with secondary students. Pacific Palisades, CA: Instructional Dynamics. (A descriptive brochure can be obtained by writing Instructional Dynamics, 1111 Galloway, Pacific Palisades, CA 90272 or by calling (310) 454-3061.)

2

Significant Contributions of Psychology to Education

"What significant contributions has psychology made to the practice of education?" could be answered by a terse "Not nearly enough!" Psychology, however, has done much to contribute and cannot be held completely accountable for what is lacking in education.

The practice of education is still considerably behind what psychology has revealed about the relationships between teaching and learning. This is partially the result of the separation that exists between university departments of psychology and education and partially the result of the fact that psychology has emerged in only the last century and is still in the process of development. Psychology has gone through a number of stages in its history.

1. Psychology emerged as a discipline.
2. To become a "respectable" science, only observable, verifiable, and replicable data were studied; thus, physiological psychology and behavioral psychology were born.
3. The effects of emotions on human behavior began to be studied.
4. Social psychology, the behavior of humans in a group, emerged.
5. Measurement, distilled in psychology, began to be a driving force in education.
6. Cognitive psychology, the scientific study of "mind events," was born.
7. Recent research on the processing done by the brain is integrating the fields of psychology, neurology, and education.

Psychology still is a relatively new discipline. The next section gives an overview of the developments in this field, with emphasis on their potential for affecting education.

Major Developments in Psychology

Only a century ago Wundt created the first psychological laboratory in Germany, where he studied elements of consciousness. (Citations are not given. They can be found in any beginning psychology text.) At the end of the last century, Pavlov, who was studying physiology, not psychology, researched the now well-known conditioned reflex. It was at the beginning of this century that psychology became a "respectable" science, focusing on phenomena that could be observed and objectively measured.

So, both physiological psychology and behavioral psychology were born and contributed important information that we use daily in education. (To raise learners' level of concern we announce a test will be at the end of this period. As a result, we may cause the students to increase their heart rate, endocrine secretion, attention, and motivation to "look, listen, and learn.")

In the first half of this century, great names emerged in the field of psychology: Watson, James, Ebbinghaus, Thorndike, Hall, Guthrie, Lewin, and Skinner, to name a few. These giants began to translate their early findings into explanations and predictors of human behavior. The notion of fear as a conditioned response became accepted. (Yet some

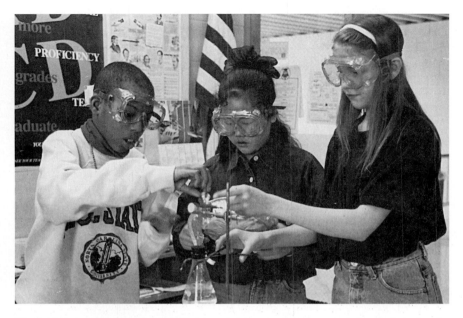

Students need to engage in active mental processing to connect new learning to their own past knowledge and experience.

still wonder why Johnny, who is failing in math, always gets a stomachache and has to go to the nurse when there is a math test.) Reinforcement theory emerged as a powerful explanation of some (not all!) human behavior. (Yet a student's smart remark that is a bid for attention is still given reenforcing, public attention by a righteous, but uninformed teacher.)

As psychologists attempted to identify a "g," or general intelligence factor, Binet and Terman made a major breakthrough with the IQ (Intelligence Quotient), as a reliable predictor of school success. Unfortunately, with our human need to eliminate ambiguity, IQ became a brand that 'destined" the fate of individuals rather than a tool to give helpful information. We now know that each learner has many IQs.

Beginning with Freud's work on the unconscious, Maslow, Rogers, and others contributed significantly to understanding human emotions as an "explainer" and predictor of certain behaviors. In the 1930s, child study groups were formed, and students were "understood." While that understanding was valuable, it contributed little to math and language teaching in the classroom, which continued with its business-as-usual, beginning-of-this-century routine.

Piaget developed insightful observations about cognition, identifying what typically occurred in stages of cognitive development, but not what teachers could do about it.

Successful learners are happy learners.

Important psychological information was stockpiling in universities and journals, but it was couched in the jargon of the psychological world, and much of it was focused on pathology. As a result, it was neither understood nor considered relevant by much of the education community. A course in psychology was required of teachers-to-be, but usually it focused on the history of psychology, big names in psychology, significant experiments in psychology, and child growth and development. Seldom did the education student see more than a dim relevance to his/her future profession. It was as if we were preparing pilots by having them study the history of flight, important names, places, and dates in the development of flight, the philosophy, sociology, and ethics of flight and then placing them in a 747 to fly a full load of passengers to Hawaii.

In fact, it was in World War II that complex behaviors of pilots came under the scrutiny of psychologists, who began to study the orchestration of action-pattern behaviors rather than single responses. To accomplish the synthesis of complex behaviors, programmed instruction was born. Much later, it was realized that teaching was also an action-performance behavior as complicated as piloting or surgery.

In the middle of this century, Benjamin Bloom chaired the group that produced the well-known *Taxonomy of Educational Objectives: Cognitive Domain*. Robert Mager's little book on *Preparing Instructional Objectives* appeared. For the first time, for many, what a teacher hoped students would accomplish was made explicit. No longer were the high-sounding but vague goals "appreciate," "enjoy," "understand," or "*really* understand" unchallenged. The outcomes of daily teaching were becoming observable and measurable. Nate Gage's *Handbook of Research on Teaching* emerged to bring together current knowledge. Still, these contributions remained small ripples that did little to rock the traditional educational boat.

Even after *Sputnik*, with the United States in a fierce competition with the then Soviet Union over the conquest of space and in a frenzy over the quality of its schools, curriculum reform rather than research on human learning was seen as the source of THE ANSWER. New math, science, and social studies curricula were spawned by federally financed programs, most of which succumbed to the toxic influence of unprepared teachers and impatient taxpayers.

New school organizational plans were tried: nongrading, team teaching, individualized instruction, modular scheduling, and the British Infant School, to name a few. But the problems in student learning refused to be "organized" away. They had to be dealt with by the obvious solution: teachers who knew how to teach to achieve a worthwhile objective, knew cause-effect relationships between teaching and learning, and who used that knowledge consciously and deliberately. It was much of the same knowledge that excellent teachers had been using intuitively since the beginning of time. Intuition, however, cannot be transmitted nor is it as consistent and reliable as research-based knowledge. Also, intuition dies with its possessor; therefore, it was not readily available to all educators nor was it accessible to beginning teachers.

Emerging from the crucible of the first three quarters of this century grew three new thrusts. First, with a new orientation, cognitive psychology now had some tools to use in the scientific study of mental events. Previously only inference and postactivity reporting, neither very reliable nor scientific, were the only evidence available. Currently, neuroscience joins with psychology, measuring cognitive-response latency in milliseconds; contrasting the operations of brain, mind, and computers; supporting and extending or, in some cases, challenging what formerly were brilliant conjectures.

A second thrust was the movement from norm-referenced to criterion-referenced tests, as well as the use of portfolios of student work. The criterion-reference tests validated students' proficiency in achieving specified objectives in education. Suddenly individual educators became accountable for results.

A third major thrust resulted from the translation of a century of psychological theory into language comprehensible to the teacher, coupled with an intensified research focus on cause-effect relationships between what a teacher did and how much students learned. Research on learning styles and teaching models revealed there was no *one* best way of teaching for *all* students and *all* situations, no matter how useful it might be in any particular set of circumstances. Teaching techniques became tools to be chosen as necessary for a particular task. Research on teaching burgeoned. More has been discovered about teaching and learning in the last two decades than was learned in preceding centuries.

Psychology and Its Influence on Education

So what have been the major contributions from psychology to education?

1.   *We now know that learning is an active, generative rather than a passive process.* A student is not a "tabula rasa" on which a teacher inscribes the heritage from previous societies, nor are students vessels into which teachers pour knowledge. As one teacher commented, "If I look on knowledge as 'pearls' which I drop into student 'bottles,' I find I am confronted daily by a room full of 'bottlenecks.'"

Psychology has shown that what a teacher does can stimulate or inhibit active processing by learners. Professional decisions involve a teacher's selecting from a large repertoire of research-based alternatives, not mastering and consistently applying a few generic teaching skills. Then, the teacher must orchestrate decisions and behaviors into a teaching-learning opportunity that is artistic, implementing what is appropriate to the particular content objective and to *these* learners in *this* situation.

2.   *Cognitive psychology has demonstrated that thinking is a process that can be enhanced.* There are observable and learnable differences between skilled and unskilled thinkers. While self-instruction in thinking works for some students, most students will learn if the skills are explic-

The "world of work" begins with imitative play as children simulate life situations.

itly taught. (Even champions benefit from coaching.) Expert teaching enables students to more nearly achieve their maximum potential in any new process or content.

3. *What students learn has a pronounced effect on their abilities to generalize, to think at higher levels, to express themselves creatively, and to make satisfying decisions.* Curricula that provide a blueprint designed to accomplish these major goals of education have emerged with greater precision in this last quarter of the century.

4. *What the teacher does is now acknowledged by both psychologists and educators as a major factor influencing whether or not students attain their maximum potential in the achievement of educational goals.* The cause-effect relationships between teaching and learning are being researched and increasingly revealed by contemporary psychologists and educators.

Rather than waiting for the final product, checking each student's progress is an important teaching function.

No longer is teaching a mysterious "laying on of hands." There now exists a basic foundation of psychological science that undergirds the art of teaching. There also exists an art of teaching that has not been defined: the virtuoso beyond the first violinist. (More virtuosos, however, emerge from first violinists than from casual "fiddlers"!)

So what has research in psychology contributed to education in this century?

1. The findings from physiological and behavioral psychology, from the early pioneers to contemporary neuroscientists, are being translated for daily use by an informed classroom teacher.

2. Learning, whether it be cognitive, affective, psychomotor, or action pattern, can be measured by observable outcomes, not inferred by wishful thinking.

3. The role of emotions and their physiological and psychological effects on learning are becoming increasingly identified, clarified, and controlled by the teacher and the learner.

4. Whether learning should be accomplished in an individual, small-group, or larger-group setting is becoming a prescription chosen from viable alternatives in the educational pharmacy. Determining learning styles and deciding on the models of teaching to be used become the results of deliberate selection by teachers *and* students.

5. Measurement and instruction are becoming stimulants complementary to each other.

6. The incremental nature of learning is accommodated by curriculum design and individual diagnosis.

7. Concepts and generalizations from content, as the springboard for thinking, creativity, problem solving and decision making, are being identified, sequenced, and then taught combining the science of psychology with the artistry of education.

Psychology and neurology are still in their infancy in their contributions to cause-effect relationships between teaching and learning, but they are robust infants with great promise as increasing contributors to the science *and* to the art of professionals in education.

Other books by this author were written to close the gap between relevant contributions of psychology and their deliberate, artistic use in the classroom. No one branch of psychology is stressed or excluded. This book, as well as many others, will assist educators to translate knowledge from all branches of psychology into effective teaching practice.

Bibliography

Anderson, J. (1985). *Cognitive psychology and its implications.* New York: W. H. Freeman.

Ashton, P. (1985). Motivation and teachers' sense of efficacy. In C. Ames and R. Ames (Eds.), *Research on motivation in education: Volume 2. The classroom milieu.* Orlando, FL: Academic Press.

Bloom, B. (1956). *Taxonomy of objectives: Cognitive domain.* New York: McKay.

Brophy, J., & Good, T. (1987). *Looking in classrooms* (4th ed.). New York: Harper & Row.

Gage, N. (1963). *Handbook of research on teaching.* Chicago, Rand McNally.

Gage, N., & Berliner, D. C. (1992). *Educational psychology.* Boston: Houghton Mifflin.

Gagné, E. D. (1985). *The cognitive psychology of school learning.* Boston: Little, Brown.

Hyde, A. A., & Bizar, M. (1989). *Thinking in context.* New York: Longman.

Mager, R. F. (1962). *Preparing instructional objectives.* Belmont, CA: Fearon.

McCown, R. R., & Roop, P. (1992). *Educational psychology and classroom practice—a partnership.* Boston: Allyn & Bacon.

Tuckman, B. W. (1992). *Educational psychology: From theory to practice.* New York: Harcourt Brace Jovanovich.

Wingfield, A. (1979). *Human learning and memory: An introduction.* New York: Harper & Row.

Wittrock, M. C. (Ed.). (1986). *Handbook of research on teaching* (3rd ed.). New York: Macmillan.

3

Questions Regarding Hunter's Contribution[1]

What's wrong with Madeline Hunter? More specifically, what's wrong with a model of teaching that increases the probability of learning by (1) identifying professional decisions teachers must make; (2) supplying research-based cause-effect relationships to support those decisions; and (3) encouraging the teacher to use data emerging from the student and the situation to augment or correct those decisions?   Doesn't knowing cause and most probable effect free teachers for creative, successful teaching? I always thought so. In fact, I still do, although I

[1]In its original form, this chapter appeared in *Educational Leadership*, February 1985.

now see that there are factors that can impinge on the correct use of this model.

Our clinical theory of instruction is based on the premise that *the teacher is a decision maker*. Because no one can tell the teacher what to *do*, our purpose is to tell teachers what to *consider* before deciding what to do and, as a result, to base teaching decisions on sound theory rather than on folklore and fantasy.

Decisions in this teacher decision-making model emerge from *propositional knowledge*: knowing what affects student learning. Propositions are generalizations, validated by psychological research, that identify behaviors that have high probability of affecting learning. Take, for instance, the following principles: "Massing practice increases speed of learning." "Distributing practice increases retention of what has been learned." These are two of several generalizations that guide a teacher's decisions about student practice. A teacher should be able to translate those propositions into *procedural knowledge* so that massed practice remains meaningful and interesting to the students. Then the teacher needs to make decisions about the length of time between distributed practice to ensure maximum learning efficiency and long-term retention. Propositions are easy to learn; creative, high-speed performance procedures are much more difficult to attain. Failing to translate propositions into procedures is a common syndrome. For example, the author's undergraduate psychology professor lectured for two solid hours on all the research that definitely proved that the average attention span is twenty minutes. A proposition may be correct, but its translation into procedure often leaves something to be desired.

Finally, this model demands *conditional knowledge*: knowing *when* to use each proposition and *why* at that moment; that is, knowing which conditions in content, student behavior, teacher behavior, and situation indicate that modifications may be necessary. *Conditional knowledge is the essence of translating science into artistry in teaching.*

Known by several names (A Clinical Theory of Instruction, ITIP, Mastery Teaching, PET, Clinical Teaching, Target Teaching, the UCLA model, the Hunter model), our model identifies decisions all teachers must make regardless of content, age or ethnicity of the learner, style of teacher, or model of teaching. It is analogous to nutrition theory. Regardless of the menu, age of the eaters, type of meal, service, or preference of the cook, meals (to be nutritious) must incorporate those nutrients that promote health. Using nutrition theory, a skilled cook can produce a variety of meals, served in a variety of ways to accommodate the tastes of the eaters. In the same way, teachers can accommodate their own teaching styles, as well as the preferences of learners, as long as those elements that promote learning are incorporated in planning, teaching, and evaluating.

Teachers must consider alternatives, then choose the most productive one, as they plan, teach, evaluate, and replan.

Myths and Misunderstandings

Let's examine some problems arising from misunderstandings and mutations that are *not* part of the basic teacher decision-making model.

1. The model is rigid and stifles creativity. On the contrary, the teacher decision-making model should provide the launching pad from which creativity can soar. All creativity is based on a basic structure from which personal originality and freedom emerge. The Taj Mahal is not a violation of the propositions of physics, engineering, and design but a beautiful manifestation of an architect's inspired translation of those propositions into reality. The propositions of this teaching model can be exquisitely used by the gifted teacher, to produce positive, satisfying results.

2. The model was created to evaluate teachers. Not at all! It was created to enhance teaching excellence. Using the model has changed many marginal teachers into effective ones, and effective teachers into masters. A skilled observer of teachers can pinpoint appropriate or inappropriate

Developing enthusiasm and skill in the arts results from "artistic" use of the decision-making model.

teaching decisions and behaviors, encouraging the former and offering productive alternatives to the latter. Rather than giving general admonitions such as "You need to tighten up your discipline—make your lessons more interesting—create more motivation in your students—develop better class routines," the model equips both the teacher observer and the teacher with knowledge, skills, and the practical assistance to attain excellence. As one teacher so beautifully put it, "Today, from my observer's feedback, I got a glimpse of the teacher I have the potential for becoming."

This model may not "save" all inadequate teachers; but if we finally accept defeat, it is not for want of research-based help so practical and attainable that the teacher must have been unwilling to use the assistance offered or incapable of doing so.

3.   *The model is great for direct teaching of content areas, but it does not apply to the arts, or to other models of teaching.* Not so! The model focuses on decision making—the decisions that underlie every mode of teaching in all content areas. In fact, teachers are not the only decision makers; any teaching decision may be delegated to the learner. Teaching models differ *only* in the source of information. Any style of teaching or learning may be used, but the teacher remains the professional primarily responsible for successful learning outcomes. The more skilled the teacher in implementing the model, the more responsible, independent, and successful learners can become, and the greater the variety of teaching and learning styles that can be used.

4.   *The model applies only to teaching in elementary school.* The model is equally effective in preschool, elementary, secondary, and university teaching, as well as in industry or the military. In fact, it applies to every human interaction that is conducted for the purpose of learning. Faculty meetings, PTA meetings, school board meetings, meetings of community groups, Scout meetings, grade-level or department meetings in schools, and learning in corporations are all improved by conscious application of the principles of human learning. An educator who can artistically implement those principles will be more successful in any situation.

5.   *The model helps teachers who are having difficulty but can contribute little or nothing to successful teachers.* Psychological research enables us to formulate learning generalizations and explain why they work. As a result, many successful teachers move from intuitive to purposeful behavior. They know what they are doing, why they are doing it, and they do it on purpose, with originality. As a result, students' learning becomes more predictable and successful. Teachers consistently express gratitude for bringing such welcome predictability to their planning and teaching. All professionals continue to grow as new research contributes to their knowledge, skills, and artistry. Teachers and administrators are no exception. In the same way that using this model speeds up learning for both slow and fast learners but does not make them equal, it also helps less able teachers to become more effective and makes more able teachers to become accomplished educational artists.

6.   *The model expects the impossible of the typical teacher.* Not at all! Even student teachers can learn to use theory to make productive teaching decisions with results that are gratifying to them, to their students, and to their supervising teachers. Knowledge and skill make all work easier to accomplish successfully. This model is not based on working harder, but on working smarter.

7.   *There has been no research to support this model.* Every proposition of this model was derived from research in human learning. Any beginning psychology text identifies the research basis for most of the propositions. The model was originally validated in Project Linkage (1973), which was funded by the California State Department of Education and implemented in a difficult Los Angeles inner-city school. Outside evaluation demonstrated substantial increases in student learning and self-esteem and in teacher satisfaction, decreases in discipline problems and vandalism. Since then, major research studies (the Napa

Skilled teachers assist with but insist on productive learning.

County NIE project, the West Orange, New Jersey project) plus many dissertations have corroborated the propositions of this model. (See the bibliography at the end of this chapter for some of these sources.) Unfortunately, many projects have attempted to evaluate results from one short training period on the use of the model or brief exposure to it without checking whether its propositions were actually translated into procedural and conditional teacher behaviors in the classroom.

8.   The model consists of a limited set of learning principles. Excellence in teaching is built on the foundation of teaching decisions that translate established principles and theories of motivation, reinforcement, retention, and practice into lesson design. From that basis, people who use the model need to know and use transfer theory to encourage students' higher-level thinking, creativity, problem solving, and decision making and help them extend their learning creatively to new situations. Teachers also need to incorporate into their teaching those principles that accelerate learning (sequence theory, level of aspiration, and so on) and promote students' positive self-esteem and their development into productive, contributing human beings. Attribution theory, one of our most recent theories of human motivation, is also a part of this dynamic model that continually adds new research to its theory base. Cognitive psychology has added information and rigor as a result of research into the operations of the brain.

Problems With Use of the Model

Problems have arisen when the teacher decision-making model was accepted but misunderstood and, therefore, inappropriately or incorrectly applied. Some *incorrect* interpretations of the model have included the following.

1.   Those seven elements of effective instruction must be in every lesson. Horrors, no! The elements (they were never called steps!) were designed to help teachers *plan.* (See chapter 8 for a list, as well as an explanation, of the seven basic elements to considered in designing lessons.) In no way can a teacher be judged on the basis of inclusion of all those elements. In fact, some lessons will incorporate only a few elements because students progress toward achievement of complex learning over a period of time. *Any observer who uses a checklist to make sure a teacher is using all seven elements does not understand the model.*

2.   If a little is good, more is better. Probably not! Teachers can overreinforce or overmotivate. Students can practice beyond what is productive and can do activities that do not facilitate their growth.

Educators must develop *conditional* knowledge to determine under what conditions procedural skills should be used. For example, if students are fatigued or bored by practice, that practice should be changed or discontinued, even though students have not mastered the skill. Such conditional knowledge is common sense—something that can be uncommon in education. Frequency counts are no more useful to teachers than to doctors. The number of times pills or surgery are prescribed does not indicate whether a doctor is making valid medical decisions. Awareness of medical propositions, procedures, and existing conditions enables a sophisticated observer to judge medical decisions and actions. In the same way, a sophisticated observer of teachers' decisions and actions can judge their appropriateness for learners, as well as the artistry in teachers' implementation of decisions.

3. *Observers judge teachers' decisions without finding out the reasons for those decisions.* Checking the reasons for a teacher's decisions will often reveal excellent professional thought processes. On the other hand, an observer frequently can see what is not visible to the teacher who is busy teaching. (The coach who is observing can see more details of what's happening in the game than can the players.) Communication between teacher and observer as to the basis for each one's thinking results in learning for both.

4. *Too much is expected too soon.* The teacher decision-making model is deceptively *simple* in conceptualization, incredibly *complex* in application. There is a quantum leap from knowing propositions to creating effective procedures. Frequently, in a workshop, teachers are exposed to sequence theory, practice theory, or whatever, and then naively expected to apply the theories magically and correctly in their "tomorrow morning" practice. Artistic performance, whether in music, writing, physical skills, or teaching, results from countless hours of practice *with coaching* designed to increase productive responses and to remediate or eliminate unproductive ones. Too frequently, teachers are not observed or coached after inservice training; consequently, they may never translate the new learning into effective teaching, or that learning appears in a form that is not as productive as it could be. Artistic and effective teaching results from a well-planned staff development program (not one session) *plus coaching*! The stages necessary to translate knowledge into effective practice have been described in other publications.

5. *Promoters of the model want to begin with teachers, bypassing administrators.* Knowledge of effective teaching should first be learned by central administrators and principals because these leaders have the potential for making the greatest difference in teaching excellence.

Administrators do not engage in daily teaching, so their skills tend to grow rusty. Also, many of their former teaching skills cannot be transmitted because they were intuitive rather than articulate and theory-based. As a result, administrators and supervisors may attempt to clone themselves and get teachers to imitate the way they "used to do it." Instead, they need to become adroit in helping teachers use their own personalities and styles to achieve excellence in the translation of theory into practice.

In addition, administrators need to demonstrate their professional skills and become models for teachers when they conduct staff meetings, parent conferences, and discipline sessions, and do occasional teaching. Otherwise, a "do as I say not as I do" situation can exist.

6. *Districts provide a one-shot or one-year exposure and then move on to a new focus.* A major problem of inservice education is the patchwork effect of a little of this and a little of that until the teacher can see no relationship between the patches. The teacher decision-making model provides a framework of cause-effect relationships into which each additional inservice session can be incorporated. Additions become a related extension or refinement of the undergirding propositions of effective teaching. Seeing the relationship between the three categories of decisions that all teachers must make—decisions about content, learning behaviors, and teaching behaviors—enables teachers to assimilate, accommodate, and use new professional information, techniques, organizational schemes, methods, and discoveries. We can't just hope that integration of professional information will occur; we must provide for it.

7. *Once teachers or administrators have been trained, they have finished learning.* A professional, whether doctor, architect, attorney, or teacher, never finishes learning that which increases professional effectiveness. Consequently, systematic and continuing renewal is essential for both teachers and administrators. In addition, even with coaching, undesirable mutations of practice can emerge, old habits spontaneously recur, and some new learning is forgotten. For these reasons, all educators need regularly scheduled renewal and revitalization.

8. *Leaders are not adequately trained.* "Trainers" take a quick crash course to acquire the propositional knowledge of the model and are then expected to teach it to others. When trainers have not had time to internalize procedural and conditional knowledge, they may not be able to translate propositions into their own teaching behaviors. In addition, they may lack the conditional knowledge of when and under what conditions to use each generalization. Frequently, beginning trainers make the error of teaching rules to govern teachers' decisions, rather than teaching generalizations on which to base decisions.

Conclusion

It is unfortunate that lack of understanding, misunderstanding, and mis-applications have resulted in some rejection and misuse of a potentially powerful model for increasing success in teaching and learning.

What is most regrettable is that I did not realize what was *really* wrong with the Hunter model, which is that I simply did not anticipate:

- The quantum leap between knowing a psychological general-ization and translating it into deliberate, artistic practice
- The temptation to accept principles of learning as absolutes—without regard for the individual teacher, individual student, and individual situation
- The possibility of treating *an* answer as *the* answer
- The blurring of the incredibly complex and subtle interactions between teachers, students, and situations when psychological theory (which can be unintelligible because of its laboratory vocabulary) is translated into simpler language
- The seduction of users into believing that excellence in teaching can be mandated and made easy, expecting dramatic results from the use of a few simple techniques
- The hunger for a quick fix, leading to belief in how-to formulas rather than the realization that achieving professional excel-lence is a long, laborious process
- That fact that failure to provide coaching and feedback for teachers and administrators during staff development is lethal (a mortal sin of those who have preached the necessity for guided practice with feedback but have not provided it)

Models are judged on their ability to guide behavior, predict out-comes, and stimulate research, not on their being the final answer. The teacher decision-making model was developed to accomplish all three purposes. If it has contributed to educators' use of research-based knowl-edge to make and implement more successful professional decisions; if it encourages, in preservice and inservice training, the constant addi-tion of new research-based propositions to guide future actions of teach-ers and administrators; if it results in increased teacher and student success and satisfaction—then it will have served its purpose in spite of "what is wrong with the Hunter Model."

Bibliography

Berg, C. A., & Clough, M. (1991). Generic lesson design: The case against. *The Science Teacher, 58*(7), 26–32.

Berg, C., Clough M., & Hunter, M. (1990). Lesson design: The wrong one for science teaching. *Educational Leadership, 48*(4), 73–78.

Donovan, J. F., Sousa, D. A., & Walberg, H. J. (1988). The impact of staff development and student achievement. *Journal of Educational Research, 80*, 348–351.

Donovan, J. F., Sousa, D. A., & Walberg, H. J. (1991). The Hunter model: A four-year longitudinal study of staff development effects. *Journal of Research and Development in Education.*

Gentile, J. R. (1988). *Instructional improvement: Summary of Madeline Hunter's essential elements of instruction and supervision.* Oxford, OH: National Staff Development Council.

Gibboney, R. A. (1987). A critique of Madeline Hunter's teaching model from Dewey's perspective. *Educational Leadership, 44*(5), 46–50.

Hunter, M. (1980). Response to Slavin. *Educational Leadership, 46*(2), 60.

Hunter, M. (1984). Comments on the Napa County, California, follow-through project. *Elementary School Journal, 87*, 173–179.

Hunter, M. (1987). Beyond rereading Dewey . . . What's next? A response to Gibboney. *Educational Leadership, 44*(5), 51–53.

Hunter, M. (1989). "Well acquainted" is not enough: A response to Mandeville and Rivers. *Educational Leadership, 46*(4), 67–68.

Hunter, M. (1990). Hunter lesson design helps achieve the goals of science instruction. *Educational Leadership, 48*(4), 79–84.

Hunter, M. (1991). Generic lesson design: The case for. *The Science Teacher, 58*(7), 26–32.

Project linkage. (1973). Report Filed with the California State Department of Education.

Mandeville, G. K., & Rivers, J. L. (1989). Effects of the South Carolina Hunter-based PET program. *Educational Leadership, 46*(4), 63–66.

Rehberg, P. (1984). The Hunter mold fits any situation. *Nebraska School Leader.* Spring 1984.

Sousa, D. A., & Donovan, J. F. (1990). Four-year study of Hunter model shows student achievement gains in some areas. *The Developer.* Oxford, OH: National Staff Development Council.

Stallings, J., & Krasavage, E. M. (1986). Program implementation and student achievement in a four-year Madeline Hunter follow-through project. *Elementary School Journal, 87,* 117–138.

4

Using Hunter's Contributions in the Real World[1]

Throughout the world, educators are being "exposed" (that word is selected deliberately) to some of the translations of psychological research into effective classroom practice that have been developed during the last two decades at the University of California, Los Angeles. Some of that research has been available for a century, but it has been buried in psychological jargon, which can be incomprehensible to a practicing educator.

Unfortunately, as is the case with so many educational issues, the "for-ers" and "agin-ers"

[1]The original version of this article appeared in *Tennessee Educational Leadership, 13*, Fall 1986.

drew up sides, with the zealots claiming THE ANSWER had been found and the reluctant dragons intoning the death of creativity and artistry in teaching. Both are operating with misinformation.

The Elements of a Decision-Making Model

Education, like medicine, law, and engineering, is an *applied* profession that synthesizes research from basic disciplines into operational decisions and practice. Just as physics, chemistry, anatomy, and physiology constitute the basic framework on which medical decisions are based, so does psychological, sociological and neurological research in human learning form the launching pad for decisions in education. Knowledge of anatomy and physiology does not give the physician specific answers. Knowledge of those fields (plus physics, chemistry, and psychology) constitutes the framework from which treatment is prescribed. Similarly, knowledge of cause-effect relationships in human learning does not tell the teacher *what* to do. It tells the teacher what s/he should know about and consider *before deciding* what to do, or what the students should do, so that what is done has the highest probability (there is never certainty with the human in education or in medicine) for successful achievement.

Consequently, ours is a *teacher decision-making model.* No one can tell a teacher what to do. We can, however, tell teachers much (not all) of what they should know and think about before deciding what to do.

Teaching, like medicine, is a relativistic, situational profession where *there are no absolutes.* There is nothing that an effective teacher *always* does or *never* does (with the one exception of never causing a student to lose dignity). Consequently, in teacher observations done for the purpose of coaching, supervision, or evaluation, a checklist can never be used unless there is a category of "not done appropriately" or "not needed in this lesson." Also, a checklist implies that mere presence of an action is enough regardless of whether it was executed well or poorly or of whether, while helpful in most lessons, it should *not* have been included in this lesson because it interfered with learning. (Here are examples of teacher actions that could interfere with learning: The teacher should *not* have let the students know the objective because it elicited a groan from students, an outcome that could have been predicted. The students should *not* have engaged in guided or independent practice because they were not ready to do the task with a reasonable degree of success. The teacher should *not* have reinforced the behavior because the students were ready to be moved to an intermittent schedule of reinforcement. No matter how adroitly the teacher uses motivation theory, it is used in error if the students are already "ready to go.") One

There is no one best way of teaching.

wonders if educators are using absolutes ("if a little is good, then more is better") because it's easier to note presence or absence of a behavior than to determine its appropriateness or effective use in a given context.

Because ours is a (not THE) decision-making model, it requires a period of gestation before it is translated into artistic and automatic practice. We now know that teaching is an action-performance profession based on knowledge that must be put into action, often at incredibly high speeds. While lesson planning can be done on "one's seat," teaching involves, at high speed, making modifications of that plan on "one's feet" as a result of perceiving data that are emerging from students and situations. This ability to change plans on one's feet requires a great deal of practice, *with coaching* designed to enhance, automate, and generate artistry in teachers' productive decisions and behaviors, as well as to remediate where indicated. Our estimate is that approximately two years are required to translate a new technique into high-speed, automatic, productive performance: to move *propositional knowledge* (the "what" of teaching) into *procedural knowledge* (the "how" of artistic and effective teaching).

The additional level of knowledge and performance that makes education a profession is *conditional knowledge*: "when?" and "why then?" should a proposition or procedure be used to make teachers' or students' actions increasingly productive?

You may note the similarity of the propositional, procedural, and conditional knowledge required of the professionals in education to the declarative, procedural, and contextual knowledge that cognitive psychologists attest are essential to problem solving, decision making, creativity, and, in fact, all higher-order thinking. Teaching is based on thinking of the highest order, which then is translated into successful professional performance.

Some General Teaching Principles

It is important to note that our model does not endorse one way of teaching. Teachers can use any model, teaching technique, procedure, or style (discovery, concept formation, cooperative learning, computer-assisted instruction, direct teaching, to name but a few), but whatever is used should be based on consideration of these factors:

- The degree of difficulty or complexity of content that is appropriate for this particular individual or group of students

As already observed, there is no one best way of teaching. Large groups or small groups are formed by students' needs.

- A successful input modality (not always the input modality preferred by each student), successful because the output of that student is perceivable to the teacher and validates that learning has occurred
- Appropriate use of those research-based principles that promote motivation to learn, increase rate and degree of learning, and contribute to the probability that learning will be retained and productively transferred to new situations that require problem solving, creativity, and decision making

That famous (or infamous) seven *elements* (as already noted, they were never called steps!) lesson design is *not* our model of teaching. A design for a lesson is a planning grid that subsequently becomes the perceivable behaviors of teacher and students and demonstrates that the three categories of decisions (content, learning behaviors, and teaching behaviors) have or have not been made productively. Lesson design is to our UCLA model of teaching as information that a cook uses is to planning a meal so that there are appropriate amounts of necessary nutrients. The meal itself is the lesson as it is conducted. Broiled chicken, baked potato, and crisp salad are a manifestation of a model of nutrition that emphasizes the research basis for serving protein, carbohydrates, vitamins, minerals, fiber, and so on. That same nutrition theory would suggest that if one has had steak and eggs for breakfast, a fruit or vegetable salad with little protein might be better for lunch. If one has had coffee and fruit juice for breakfast, protein is indicated for lunch. Sometimes, certain elements should *not* be included in a lesson. If a teacher checks for understanding too soon, mistakes can become set.

Lesson design simplifies planning the complex decision-making process of teaching by suggesting seven generic activities the teacher can use *as needed*. These elements are to be included or excluded deliberately. They encourage creativity and diversity rather than constrict teaching.

So what do we do to increase the probability that all educators (not just teachers) will use psychological theory productively?

1. We make sure they have opportunities to acquire research-based propositional knowledge about teaching-learning relationships.
2. With practice *and coaching*, we help educators translate this cognitive knowledge into performance behaviors that result in more productive classroom learning, as well as being used in staff meetings, conferences with parents, management of discipline, supervision and evaluation of teachers, and work with school boards. All of these activities require procedural and conditional knowledge and can reveal the acquisition and internalization of propositional knowledge.

3. With practice *and coaching*, we help educators develop the sensitivity to know when a proposition or procedure applies to a given learner or group in a specific situation and when that proposition or procedure would be inappropriate.

4. We do not create absolutes of "thou shalt" or "indices of the effective teacher." (Often indices are merely correlates: effective teachers smile more—they have more to smile about!) We do not check for presence or absence of any behavior (for example, level of questions, equal turns to recite, percentage of teacher-talk to student-talk) in lieu of making an informed judgment about the appropriateness of *those* questions, *these* turns, *that* teacher-talk, *this* instructional objective for *these* students in this situation.

In short, we do not submit to the tyranny of the short right answer in the most complex process in the world—teaching and learning.

Conclusion

So, to use or not to use the Hunter model? The answer is NO if, through misinformation, teachers become robots who feel they should proceed through certain steps whether or not all the elements are needed in this lesson or for these students; who feel they must "cover" the material; who are evaluated by the presence or absence of checklists, rather than by the appropriateness of their decisions or actions for these students in this classroom; who are expected to use skills they haven't had an opportunity to learn through district-sponsored staff development programs (rather than donated vacation time); or who haven't had the time or opportunity to practice, with coaching, in order to develop artistry and proficiency; in short, where pseudo-use of the Hunter model becomes constricting rather than freeing.

The answer is YES if it means that a teacher becomes a decision-making professional who selects content that is achievable with appropriate effort by the student; who gives students opportunities to develop many learning modalities and styles; who checks learning achievement before moving on; who accelerates learning through the use of appropriate principles of learning and effective teaching techniques; who uses his/her own personality and commitment to make learning a satisfying outcome of school experiences; who, with inservice training, practice, and coaching continues to increase proficiency in both the science and the art of teaching throughout professional life.

The decision is yours. Make it with professional integrity.

Section

2

Decisions
About
Content

Curricular content, the *"what* is to be learned,"
must be determined before the decision about
"how students will learn it." In the same way,
the menu of a meal must be determined before its
cooking and serving can be begun. Unfortunately,
the plethora of already-prepared materials tempts
teachers to start with the *how*, using these materials without considering more than vague positive outcomes in general academic areas. This
same diffusion of intent and effort can exist in
the planning for learning of cognitive processes,

affective outcomes, and psychomotor skills, which also are part of the curriculum.

Chapter 5 assists teachers in making more precise decisions about what is to be learned, its value to the student, and ways of increasing the probability of successful student achievement by ensuring that the level of difficulty of the task is appropriate for each student at a particular point in time. By "factoring out" simpler concepts and by identifying enabling, prerequisite behaviors and then teaching them, teachers can immeasurably enhance the probability of students' acquiring more complex processes.

Chapter 6 emphasizes the necessity for developing *student-generated* meaning, versus "teacher telling," in order for them to understand the concepts, generalizations, and discriminations that are essential for functioning in our complex society: these are the "building blocks" of thinking. Techniques for teaching these higher-level thinking skills are described and illustrated in this chapter.

Chapter 7 is focused on ways of *teaching to an objective*, to ensure that learning is achieved with greater probability. It describes how objectives can add precision, rather than the constraint of "what one *should* do," to learning opportunities that reflect students' needs and teachers' styles.

This section on curriculum concludes with chapter 8, which covers that famous (or infamous) Hunter lesson design—the elements of effective instruction that, because of their power in producing well-designed lessons, unfortunately became a checklist of "what teachers must do." This outcome was *never* intended. The elements were intended as a guide to what must be considered in designing lessons and, as a result of that thoughtful consideration, either included as facilitating learning or excluded as unnecessary in a lesson. The elements, when the research base for their functions is understood, become a planning guide for effective teaching.

5

Curricular Decisions, Task Analysis, and Diagnosis

Curricular decisions affect what specific objectives are taught daily in the classroom and how attainment of these objectives by students is to be measured. This chapter explores the relationship between overall curriculum goals, daily classroom learning opportunities, and diagnosis.

Curricular Decisions

Major content decisions about what is to be learned must be made in two categories: philosophic and scientific. In the conduct of education, each category is critically important.

Philosophic Decisions Determine "Ends" in Education

The first category of decisions to be made are philosophically based. They determine which general learnings and goals will compose the formal and informal curriculum, the "what" of teaching.

Decisions in this category are usually derived from values and beliefs of a society rather than from scientific information. On the basis of values and beliefs, curricular goals are set and defended as being worthwhile by members of a culture. We value U.S. history, decision making, the arts, reading, math, and other such subject areas, both for their worth in themselves and for their potential for transfer to promote the individual's achievement and satisfaction throughout life.

Reading is valued as giving the learner enjoyment and access to accumulated knowledge. Math is valued as being the key to quantitative understandings necessary in life. Learning about other cultures is valued for its contribution to one's appreciation and respect for them. Health education is valued as fostering one's well-being. Examples of philosophically based goals of education are "a valid and positive self-concept," "responsible freedom," "respecting the rights of others," "decision-making skills," "patriotism," "competence in the 3Rs." Other cultures could have different goals: "deference to authority," "being seen and not heard," "placing the state ahead of the person."

From goals that reflect the values of a society, the school curriculum is extrapolated: a feat of educational engineering that provides a blueprint for achievement of the desired learnings. From this blueprint, a teacher must derive the major *instructional objectives* for which that teacher is responsible.

Instructional objectives have two primary attributes. One is a precise description of a cognitive, affective, or psychomotor learning that is the intended outcome of the student's effort. The other attribute of an instructional objective is perceivable student behavior, or the product of that behavior, that demonstrates or validates successful accomplishment.

Examples
The learner will write a descriptive paragraph (cognitive).
The learner will choose poetry for leisure reading (affective).
The learner will throw a ball from first to second base (psychomotor).
Instructional objectives also may include the conditions under which the student's perceivable behavior or product will occur and the criteria by which that learning will be judged as successful.

Example
Given 15 minutes, the learner will solve two-step word problems with 90 percent accuracy.

Curriculum goals are those considered worthwhile by each culture.

Scientific Decisions Determine "Means" in Education

A second category of decisions in curricular design is derived from a scientific rather than a philosophic base: the category involves the selection of a sequence of learnings. To determine sequence, cause-effect relationships revealed by research in learning are specified and incorporated into teaching decisions and behaviors. The result is that students are helped to acquire complex generalizations based on the acquisition of simpler concepts and generalizations. Analyzing cause-effect relationships and using psychological principles and research increase the probability of a student's achievement of specific objectives that lead to the more general goals that have been philosophically determined.

Neither the philosophic nor the scientific category of decisions is the more important. The finest goals are of no use if they are not achieved, and the most effective achievement is to no avail if the goals are not worth the effort.

The Nature of Task Analysis

This section of the chapter, while reminding the reader first to examine and validate goals and objectives in terms of their worthwhileness, focuses on *task analysis*, a critical element in the application of science to the sequence of learning. Task analysis is the process of breaking down complex learnings into simpler learnings and then sequencing those learnings for efficient and effective student achievement.

A further application of science to the *how* (pedagogy) instead of to the *what* (curriculum) of teaching is based on the teacher's use of validated principles of learning in order to "bring it off." A few skills in using those principles have been described in other chapters of this book (chapters 9 to 22). Many are described elsewhere (see the bibliography in chapter 1) and will not be discussed in this book.

In the past, task analysis remained in the domain of the curriculum builder, who often neglected it or subsumed it under the umbrella of "learnings and activities necessary to achieve ____." Now the process of task analysis is accepted as being an essential component of all successful instructional planning. Rather than remaining an esoteric skill of the curriculum theorist, task analysis has become an important tool of the teacher, essential to the use of a curriculum guide and to daily instructional decisions.

Teachers use information from a task analysis in three ways: for planning curricular sequences, for initial diagnosis, and for ongoing diagnosis. These are not discrete functions and more than one may be occurring at the same time, but for the purpose of examining them, each will be considered separately.

Task Analysis for Planning Curricular Sequences

Curricular goals must be translated into major learning outcomes. From the major, long-range outcomes, the component or subordinate objectives are derived. Component objectives must be ordered in some sequence of learnings that, more effectively than random experiences, makes the achievement of major objectives possible and even probable. Component objectives must then be translated into plans for weekly and daily learning opportunities in order for students to accomplish the long-range objectives.

A task analysis increases in specificity as it narrows focus from broad goals to daily teaching objectives. Specificity is essential to a teacher's planning to ensure students' efficient and successful achievement at any point in the curricular sequence. While a task analysis that is related to major curricular objectives can be done by the curriculum specialist or someone removed from the classroom, the classroom teacher must be actively involved in the relationship between a general curricular task analysis and the more detailed task analysis that is essential in daily planning for a class. For example, the curriculum specialist may correctly schedule paragraph writing before introductory or concluding paragraphs. The teacher, however, must make decisions daily as to which component skills the students should be working on, such as making transitions from one sentence to the next, using descriptive words, employing a variety of sentence patterns, or generating topic sentences.

Task Analysis for Initial Diagnosis and Prescription

To establish the most productive focus of the teaching and learning effort, each student's current achievement must be diagnosed. It is wasteful for both teacher and student to devote time and energy to a learning that already has been achieved and needs no more practice. It is equally indefensible to expend time and energy on a learning task that is impossibly difficult because simpler learnings, essential to achievement, have not been mastered. A task analysis constitutes the foundation for the diagnostic activity or instrument used to reveal which components (subskills) of the intended learning have been achieved by a student and which components remain to be mastered.

Results from a diagnosis based on a task analysis tell the teacher where to start and who needs to learn what. The results do not necessarily mean something different for every student but learnings that are at the appropriate level of difficulty for each.

Task Analysis for Ongoing Diagnosis

Initial diagnosis *may* (not necessarily *should*) be accomplished by instruments or activities designed by someone removed from the classroom of students being diagnosed. *Ongoing* diagnosis, however, whether formal, informal, or inferential (based on a teacher's prior experience with similar students), is best conducted by the teacher who is working with those students. Successful ongoing diagnosis requires that the teacher continuously use the information generated by a task analysis (1) to monitor student progress so that remediation, if necessary, will be provided as soon as it is indicated; (2) to probe for what is missing in an unsuccessful student performance in order to build in that missing component so that success is possible; and (3) to respond when students' achievements suggest accelerated pacing. Consequently, the teacher must be skilled in the process of task analysis, as well as in the use of the information that results from it.

Steps in a Task Analysis

From a general philosophic goal in education, the curriculum identifies a major objective that contributes to the achievement of that philosophic goal. The steps in a task analysis of a major objective are illustrated below, using an example from teaching writing.

Example
Goal: Effective Communication

Major Objective: The learner will express him/herself skillfully and artistically in expository writing.

1.   State an objective that narrows the major objective to one for which a particular teacher has responsibility.

Example
The learner will write a paragraph.

2.   State qualifiers (which would change from primary through elementary to secondary students) that accurately describe to a fellow professional the criteria or attributes of a student response, performance, or product that would constitute evidence of successful achievement of that objective. (Reasonable precision does not mean nitpicking.)

Example
The paragraph will contain a topic sentence and five or more related sentences that support the topic sentence. Conventions of spelling, punctuation, capitalization, indentation, and correct grammar will be incorporated.

3.   State the entry level or baseline of your task analysis: the learning or skills you infer are already possessed by the student. If your inference proves to be incorrect, you can redo the task analysis below this baseline later.

Example
The student can write a sentence.

4.   List essential components of the target objective: what the student must know or be able to do to move from the baseline to successful achievement. There are several ways of identifying these components.

   a. Do the final task yourself and describe what you are doing or thinking. It often helps to "think aloud in slow motion" about what you are doing.

   b. Observe or "image" in your mind someone else doing the task, and record what s/he is doing at each point.

   c. Examine or "image" the final product and infer what the student must have done or thought about to accomplish it.

   d. Check your task analysis for inferred components that are nonobservable behaviors but that the student must have performed internally: e.g, knowing what choices are available, selecting a topic, having information before writing, weighing possibilities.

   e. Subject each component you have identified to question and examination by asking "Could you do the final task without having achieved this component?" By doing this, you factor out *essential* components from those that may be highly desirable or related but not essential. While all components contribute to a quality product, if time runs out (and it frequently does), essential components need to be learned first. Continuing the example, here are some essential components for the objective of writing a paragraph.

Example

The learner will write a paragraph.

Example of essential components for the objective include—

- Select a topic
- Generate and write five or more sentences related to the topic
- Sequence sentences in some logical order with necessary transitions
- Generate a topic sentence
- Proofread for conventions of spelling, punctuation, grammar, word choice, capitalization, form

Here are examples of desirable, but not absolutely essential skills:

- Using a variety of sentence patterns
- Using descriptive language
- Using "model" handwriting

5. Separate components into a sequence of dependent and independent learnings: dependent components refer to learnings for which teachers and students have no choice of sequence because learnings must logically be acquired in a certain order (for example, sentences before paragraphs, addition and subtraction before multiplication and division). Independent components are those learnings where students and/or teachers may choose whether they be acquired at the beginning, end, or in the middle (for example, descriptive words before or after variety in sentence pattern). Note that the order of execution of the skills needed to achieve an objective is not necessarily the order in which they must be learned. (For example, you can learn to put on your shoes before or after you learn to put on your socks, but when you get dressed, your socks must go on first.)

6. Develop a sequence in which dependent components are arranged in their required order and independent components are placed in an order according to interest, materials, schedule, and so on. (Beware of falling into the trap of planning *how* you would teach those components rather than what is to be learned. The *how* comes later.)

Example

Here is an example of dependent sequence of components:

First: Decide on specific topic or main idea of the paragraph.

Second: Write sentences related to that focus and from those sentences, generate a topic sentence *or* generate a topic sentence and then write supporting sentences. These two tasks can occur in either order.

Third: Check for transitions and the logic of sentence sequence in the paragraph.

Fourth: Proofread and edit.

Here is an example of an independent sequence of components (done in any order): practice generating transitions and conventions of form, punctuation, spelling, and correct language usage. These skills may be learned prior to paragraph writing. They may then be incorporated in the initial writing of paragraphs but usually are attended to at the proofreading stage.

Designing Diagnostic Activities

The next instructional function is to create diagnostic activities, using the components determined in the task analysis.

A diagnostic activity enables the teacher to identify the components that each student already has achieved and to determine what remains to be learned.

1.   Translate every component of the instructional objective between the baseline and successful achievement into a "can" question.

Example
Can the learner—

- Select a topic, or does s/he have the information necessary to respond to a given topic?
- Generate sentences related to the topic?
- Arrange sentences with some logical sequence and necessary transitions?
- Generate a topic sentence?
- Proofread for conventions of spelling, punctuation, grammar, word choice, capitals, form?

2.   Determine whether achievement of each component will be validated by *direct or indirect* behavior that demonstrates achievement (stating, writing, selecting, identifying, discussing, producing, correcting).

Direct Examples
- A *process* performed by the students that demonstrates possession of the *necessary* skills. Example: The learner will state the topic and then generate five sentences related to the topic.

- A *product* that validates that the student knows it or has done it (written sentences, reports, tests, models, paragraph, composition). Example: The learner will write a paragraph that includes specified elements.

Indirect Example
The learner will select the topic sentence that goes with a paragraph.

3.   Conduct a diagnostic activity. The teacher will use students' processes or products that yield answers to the "can" questions. This activity should identify the disparity between what the student can do and what s/he needs to learn to do—in other words, what needs to be taught.

4.   Use the diagnostic information. When diagnosis reveals that a student has *not* achieved an assumed baseline objective (for example, expressing ideas in sentences), a teacher may need to do a further task analysis of that lacking component to identify enabling objectives that will help the student to achieve the prior, essential component.

Example
The learner will discriminate sentences from nonsentences.
The objective of discriminating sentences from nonsentences is not essential to writing a paragraph, but it is enabling to students who have a difficult time recording their thoughts.

To identify enabling behaviors, think of activities that do not necessarily occur in a satisfactory performance, but that could logically be assumed to contribute to the probability of satisfactory performance. In the writing example, the enabling activities could be simpler communications, performances, or products such as orally communicating in sentences, and generation of different words that mean about the same thing and words that mean the opposite or generation of expressive verbs such as *yelled, shouted, hissed, whispered* (instead of always using *said*).

5.   Plan learning opportunities. Using the results of a diagnostic activity, the teacher plans appropriate instructional activities. These might include cooperative learning groups, grouping students for teacher instruction, or meeting individual needs within the total group by providing self-instructional materials, assigning additional practice at home, or any other activities that will lead to acquisition of the target objectives at the appropriate level of difficulty for each student. If task analysis and diagnosis are accurate and *principles of learning are skillfully incorporated in teaching*, student achievement becomes as probable as it is possible for a teacher to make it.

Direct teaching can build the component skills necessary for creative endeavor.

Examples: Curricular Goals, Task Analysis, and Diagnosis

The following are examples of two curricular goals or objectives, valued by our society and relevant to every class, on which a task analysis has been performed. They illustrate concretely the results of the principles described in this chapter.

Objective 1

The learner works productively on a self-selected or teacher-assigned task without direct teacher supervision.

Baseline:
Assume nothing!

Component Objectives:
The learner—

1. Has demonstrated skills necessary to do the task without assistance
2. Selects an appropriate place to work
3. Gets necessary materials
4. Gets started quickly
5. Follows directions, procedures, and rules for task
6. Works so that others can continue working
7. Works without unnecessary distractions
8. Returns to the task quickly after an interruption
9. Conserves materials and uses materials appropriately
10. Goes to appropriate sources for help (self, materials, peers, teacher)

The arts provide excellent opportunities for productive, self-directed, independent work.

11. Completes the task according to appropriate criteria
12. Records any data needed at completion of the task
13. Returns materials appropriately
14. Discriminates times when choices can be made
15. Makes an appropriate choice when s/he has the opportunity to do so
16. Moves to an appropriate next activity
17. Moves around the room so that others can continue working
18. Takes care of personal needs according to class procedures

Objective 2

The learner will participate productively in a discussion. (A discussion is defined as a verbal exchange to expand or defend two or more points of view.)

Baseline:
The learner can speak so as to be understood by other participants.

Component Objectives:
The learner will—

1. Demonstrate that s/he has information
2. Speak so s/he can be heard in a group, using comprehensible language
3. Take turns and stay on topic
4. Make responses (verbal or nonverbal) that indicate s/he has heard and understood others
5. Build on what others say—disagree agreeably
6. Ask questions to clarify and respond to others' questions
7. Support ideas
8. Synthesize (connect ideas)
9. Summarize
10. Change or maintain position when others' contributions indicate this is appropriate
11. Use appropriate body language
12. Redirect discussion when it strays off topic
13. Chair a discussion

When the components of a task analysis are expressed as instructional objectives, they indicate what must be learned to achieve the major objective, as well as what must be diagnosed. For both of the sample objectives just described, the diagnostic instrument may be an informed observer who records the results of seeing students perform that tasks.

All of the components are learned skills. (Students usually don't come equipped with them.) That which is learned can be taught and teaching is our business!

Bibliography

Arom, A. B. (1988). *What current research in teaching and learning says to the practicing teachers*. Robert Karplus Lecture. St. Louis: National Science Teachers Association National Convention.

Cruickshank, D. R. (1987). *Reflective teaching*. Reston, VA: Association of Teacher Educators.

Hunter, M. (1992). *How to change to a nongraded school*. Alexandria, VA: Association for Supervision and Curriculum Development.

Hunter, M. (1984). Knowing, teaching, and supervising. In P. L. Hosford (Ed.), *Using what we know about teaching* (pp. 169–192). Alexandria, VA: Association for Supervision and Curriculum Development.

Mager, R. F. (1962). *Preparing instructional objectives*. Palo Alto, CA: Fearon.

McPeck, J. E. (1981). *Critical thinking and education*. New York: St. Martin's.

Porter, A., & Brophy, J. (1988). Synthesis of research on good teaching: Insights from the work of the Institute for Research on Teaching. *Educational Leadership, 45*(8), 74-85.

Rubin, L. J. (1984). *Artistry in teaching*. New York: Random House.

6

Teaching Concepts, Generalizations, and Discriminations

All higher-order thinking is based on the thinker's possession and use of concepts, generalizations, and discriminations. Thinking is a performance behavior that results from a student's having learned both the necessary content information and the thinking skill or process involved. The ability to apply learning to solving a new situation (perform by thinking) entails the use of concepts and generalizations rather than recall of specific items of information. To generalize correctly also requires the ability to discriminate between the situations where a generalization is applicable and where it is not.

Concepts, Generalizations, and Discriminations Defined

A *concept* is the name of a category (chair, red, mammals, courage) that includes many perceptively different members. For example, the concept "chair" encompasses any specific piece of furniture with a back and a seat at about knee height on which only one person typically sits. The concept of "mammal" encompasses every animal that has mammary glands and hair no matter how different a "specific instance" (bats, whales) may appear.

A *generalization* is a statement expressing relationships between or among concepts. To generalize is to treat things that may appear to be different as if they are the same. A generalization may be a rule, law, principle, probability statement, or sentence defining critical attributes. Here are some examples: "Thrones are the official chairs of rulers." "Elephants, whales, and mice are all mammals."

A *discrimination* is the identification of attributes or characteristics of a specific instance that alert the student that this is not a member of the category, although it may appear to qualify in many respects. To discriminate is to correct the possibility of overgeneralizing or generalizing incorrectly. To discriminate is to treat things that may appear

Higher order thinking depends on students' ability to apply concepts and generalizations.

to be the same as if they are different. Here are some examples: "A chair is not the same as a stool, even if the stool has a back." "A porpoise and a fish are not in the same class of animals, even though they both live in water." "The letter b is not the same as the letter d."

To generalize and to discriminate are mirror images of each other. Both are based on accurate concept formation and the acquisition of valid generalizations.

The critical attributes of a concept must be understood by the student before s/he can make valid generalizations or discriminations. The identification of the critical attributes may be articulated or nonarticulated (intuitive) on the part of the student. Forming generalizations or discriminations results from the student's perceptions of presence or absence of the critical attributes that make something what it is. For example: "A circle is a continuous line with all points equidistant from the center." "A square is a four-sided, closed figure with equal sides and equal angles." An additional critical attribute is that a circle or a square is two dimensional; therefore, a ball or a cube will not qualify. Critical attributes must be perceived either intuitively or consciously by the student if s/he is to discriminate a square and a circle from a rectangle or an ellipse.

A generalization expresses the relationship among concepts. The knowledge and understanding of the concepts that are related in a generalization are essential first steps before the generalization can be understood and subsequently applied to a new situation.

To validate that a student possesses a concept requires that the student discriminate, generate, or select new instances of that concept (for example, identify additional instances of a square or circle in the environment). This extension of understanding is called "transfer" or "elaboration" and creates a network of relationships in the student's long-term memory. Networks are more efficiently stored and retrieved from memory than are single instances.

The Teacher's Role in Promoting Critical Thinking

Higher-order thinking requires the application of concepts, generalizations, and discriminations to new situations: a situation to which the person does not have a ready or automatic response. If we wish more complex thinking to occur, we need to learn how to help students acquire and use concepts, generalizations, and discriminations.

It is important to stress that "teaching" includes all modes of learning for which the teacher is responsible: direct instruction; deductive, inductive, or discovery learning; cooperative learning; or individualized learning. It includes the use of computers, prepared materials, teacher-written materials, or audiovisual materials. A teacher plans for and encourages students' utilization of all modes of learning. The *concept* of teaching certainly includes more than direct instruction. (Incidentally, this is a concept many educators still have not acquired.)

At times, we may plan for students to discover concepts, generalizations, and discriminations by themselves. At other times, we use direct teaching to explain them so that students are guided to generate meaning and relationships, in order that these "thinking tools" are more predictably acquired. The important issue is not *how* concepts, generalizations, and discriminations are acquired but that they are internalized. That achievement is primarily the result of the professional skill of the teacher, regardless of the mode of students' acquisition.

The Teaching of Concepts

A concept is the name of a category rather than a specific instance. To develop a concept, regardless of whether we teach it directly or students discover it, we must first identify for ourselves the critical attributes or functions of the concept that make that concept what it is—that is, determine which members are included or excluded from the concept or category. "A square is a closed figure with four equal sides and four right angles." Note that the critical attributes of a square are themselves concepts: closed, figure, four, equal, sides, right angles.

For each of these concepts, a student must generate meaning and then discriminate it from other similar concepts: four as opposed to three or five, right angle as opposed other angles, equal as opposed to unequal. At the beginning of learning, we need to present concepts in their simplest form, possibly a line drawing of a square so that there will be no distraction from the critical attributes. (That is why very simple examples are used in this chapter.) Then the square must be discriminated from a trapezoid, a rectangle, or other parallelograms, regardless of size, color, position, thickness of lines, and so on.

The critical attribute of the concept "compromise" is that each party gets *some* of what s/he wants but not *all* of what s/he wants. If a boy wants to use the car every Saturday and his father wants him to work in the yard, it is a compromise if some Saturdays the boy gets the car and some Saturdays he works in the yard. The number of "yard" vs. "car" Saturdays is not the critical attribute. There could be a ratio of one-to-three in a month, or there could be a ratio of two-to-two. This is not important to the concept "compromise."

Sometimes it is not possible to articulate the critical attribute. Even linguists have not specified the critical attribute of a sentence in a way that we can transmit it in a simple form to a student. In such cases, through the use of examples, we have to develop an intuitive (nonarticulated) knowledge of the concept. "The ball is in the tree" is a sentence. "The ball" or "in the tree" or "although the ball is in the tree" are not sentences.

Helping students discuss patterns and relationships is an essential component to "learning how to think," extrapolate, and solve problems.

The Teaching of Generalizations

Generalizations are declarative sentences that include rules, laws, principles, statements of critical attributes, and probability statements. A generalization expresses the relationship between two or more concepts. For example: "Dogs can be friendly." "People live in houses." "Periods go at the end of declarative sentences." "A response that is reinforced increases in probability or frequency."

In order that students effectively acquire a generalization, initial examples of that generalization must be simple, unambiguous, and consistent. (See chapter 15.) Then the student should encounter a wide variety of situations in which that generalization is held constant. Only after the generalization is well learned should exceptions be introduced.

Let's look at a very simple generalization: "Two of anything plus two more of the same thing equals four of that thing." We represent this generalization by $2 + 2 = 4$. To help students learn that generalization, examples should hold the generalization constant but present it in the widest possible variety of circumstances, starting with concrete visuals. "2 oranges plus 2 oranges equal 4 oranges." "2 books + 2 books = 4 books." "2 days + 2 days = 4 days." "2 minutes + 2 minutes = 4 minutes." "2 ideas + 2 ideas = 4 ideas."

When students are learning the generalization that the letters *c-a-t* in that order spell the word *cat*, we introduce "cat" with a picture on the page and then only the word on the top and in the middle of the page. The student associates the letters with the concept "cat." Eventually the student encounters and recognizes the word *cat* in capital letters, in manuscript, in italics, in cursive, written on book jackets, on billboards, and in books.

When we wish the student to *discover* the generalization, we carefully prepare the examples. To teach "When two or more subjects are joined by *or*, the subject closest to the verb determines the verb form," we introduce examples such as these: "Dogs or a cat *is* in the house." "A cat or dogs *are* in the house." "He or they or I *am* going." "I or they or he *is* going." "He or I or they *are* going." We use the same subjects but vary the order, to focus the student on the relationship between the verb and subject closest to it.

If we plan for students to acquire this same generalization by direct teaching rather than by discovery, we may use the same examples, but we would state the rule rather than have students discover it. "When two or more subjects are connected by *or*, the subject closest to the verb determines the form of the verb." Students' practice will continue with examples that make obvious the relationship of the verb form to the closer subject: "Harry or I *am* responsible." "Carrots or celery *is* in the soup." "Either you or he *goes* with me."

The Teaching of Discriminations

Making a discrimination is a process that requires the *opposite* kind of thinking from generalizing. You discriminate when a new situation, idea, or object seems to be the same, but you discern it does not possess the required critical attributes. It is a process that prevents over-generalizations. Discrimination requires recognizing the presence of an attribute that indicates that this is *not* an instance of that category. Consequently, the student should treat things that appear similar as if they are different (the word *hit* vs. *kit*, the animal bat vs. the animal bird, the colon (:) vs. the semicolon (;), the statement "He *or* I am going" vs. "He *and* I are going").

To help students learn to *discriminate* between similar concepts and generalizations (chair, stool), we hold surrounding situations and conditions constant but vary the presence or absence of the critical attributes that indicate it *is* or *is not* an instance of that concept or generalization. Students need to avoid guessing, but instead they should support or challenge the correctness of their discriminative judgment by verbally identifying the attribute being used. This "generalization" will be clarified by the following examples.

To discriminate between the concepts of "addition" and "subtraction," we would hold everything constant except the critical attribute that indicates which operation is appropriate. (Combining quantities is the critical attribute of the *concept* of addition; separating parts from a whole is the critical attribute of the *concept* of subtraction.) "How many pennies would you have if you had 3 pennies and found 2?" in contrast to "How many pennies would you have if you had 3 pennies and lost 2?" "How many problems would you have done if you finished 15 and then did another 10?" in contrast to "How many problems would you still have to finish if you had to do 15 problems and had already done 10?" Key words (for example, *all together, total, remainder, have left*) are *not* appropriate discriminators!

To develop the discrimination between the generalization that "*c-a-t* spells cat" and other similar letter configurations, we might ask students to find the name of the animal that says "meow" in the following: *can, cap, car, cat, cab, cad.* To test young students' ability to discriminate between the concepts of "cat" and "skunk," we would need to hold the color and setting constant by using pictures of a black-and-white cat and a skunk.

To develop the discrimination of which of the subjects connected by *or* is closest to the verb, we might ask students to circle the word that determines the verb form and cross out other subjects that have no effect. To develop the discrimination of that rule from the rule that "Whenever two or more subjects are joined by *and*, the verb is always plural," we would use sentences such as "He *or* I ____ going" and "He *and* I ____ going" and then have the students select the correct verb form.

When you teach a concept (category with members who possess stipulated critical attributes) or a generalization (a statement that expresses the relationships between concepts), you keep constant the critical attributes, but you vary the situation as widely as possible.

When you teach a discrimination, you hold the situations constant, but vary the presence or absence of the critical attributes. Knowing what something is, is knowing what it is not.

Which of these concepts or discriminations would you teach first and why? See if you can create a generalization that a teacher could apply to any situation. (No one has done this so far. We suspect it is a relational and situational decision.)

1. Would you first teach a "square" in a variety of situations, or would you begin with a square and a nonsquare?
2. A colon, or a colon and a semicolon?
3. Democracy, or democracy and dictatorship?

Concept development can be verbal or nonverbal.

4. Red, or red and not red?

5. Addition, or addition and subtraction?

6. Dependent clauses, or dependent and independent clauses?

Specify your reasons and see if you can create the generalization that would help teachers decide.

Generalizations About Teaching

Problems exist in teachers' use of generalizations about teaching, derived from psychology. These problems arise because either (1) those generalizations have not been well enough learned so that they transfer positively to new situations requiring their use or (2) the discriminating attributes have not been taught so that teachers can differentiate between times when a particular principle applies and should be used and times when that principle should not be used. Although teaching situations may appear to be the same, there are perceivable clues that signify they are different. As a result of lack of discriminations, generalizations in teaching can become false absolutes (for example, "You should always _____") and teachers can become "direction followers" rather than professional decision makers.

Let's look at an example of a way we might apply this generalization from the psychology of learning: "mass practice for fast learning; distribute practice for long retention (remembering)." The concepts of "fast learning" and "long retention" are familiar to teachers. The critical attribute of the concept of "practice" is doing something again to increase accuracy, fluency, or retention of the information or skill. The critical attribute of the concept "massed" is practicing several times without intervening activities. The critical attribute of the concept "distributed" is that other activities occur between practice periods.

Using this generalization as one *thinks* about teaching requires discrimination of whether, at this point, learning needs to become more accurate or fluent or whether those learnings have been reasonably achieved and the objective now is students' making the learning automatic and/or remembering the learning. As an example, when the concept of "square" is being learned, students will mass practice, identifying squares of various sizes, shapes, colors, in a variety of contexts. Once students have learned the concept "square," *distributed* practice in identifying squares will be utilized, with longer and longer time intervals between practices so that automaticity and permanence of learning are achieved.

To teach the rule about "subjects joined by *or*," we would give students several sentences with different subjects and varying numbers of subjects, holding the *or* that joins those subjects constant (massed practice). Then we might review the learning the next day, skip a day, review, skip several days, review only occasionally to establish long remembering (distributed practice). Eventually, we would have students practice discriminating between sentences where subjects were joined by *or* and sentences when subjects were joined by *and*.

Summary

To teach a concept, we identify (if possible) the critical attributes of that concept and present the attributes in a wide variety of situations. The greater the variety of situations, the more effective the learning of that concept and the more accurately that learning will transfer to new situations.

To teach a generalization, we make sure students understand the embedded concepts and the relationships among them. Then we hold the generalization constant in the widest possible variety of situations. The greater the variety of situations, the more mental operations on the part of the student and the more memorable and transferable that generalization will become.

To teach discriminations, we hold the situation constant and vary only the presence or absence of the critical attributes of that concept or generalization that the student must use to make the discrimination. The more discriminations a student makes when surrounding situations are similar, the more quickly the discriminations will be learned and the longer they will be remembered.

Teaching concepts, generalizations, and discriminations effectively so that students generate meaning for themselves is a major and essential contribution to students' abilities to think creatively, to solve problems, and to make responsible, satisfying decisions: the goal of all education.

Bibliography

Baron, J. B., & Steinberg, R. J. (Eds.). (1987). *Teaching thinking skills: Theory and practice.* New York: W. H. Freeman

Beyer, B. K. (1984). Improving thinking skills: A practical approach. *Phi Delta Kappan, 65,* 556–560.

Beyer, B. K. (1985). Critical thinking revisited. *Social Education, 49,* 268–269.

Ennis, R. H. (1985). Critical thinking and the curriculum. *National Forum, 45,* 28–31.

Gagné, E. D. (1985). *The cognitive psychology of school learning.* Boston: Little, Brown.

Glover, J. A., Ronney, R. R., & Brunay, R. H. (1991). *Cognitive psychology for teachers.* New York: Macmillan.

Haller, E. P., Child, D. A., & Walberg, H. J. (1988). Can comprehension be taught?: A quantitative synthesis of "metacognitive" studies. *Educational Researcher, 17*(9), 5–8.

Hunter, M. (1978). *Teach for transfer.* El Segundo, CA: TIP Publications.

Jones, B. F. (1986). Quality and equality through cognitive instruction. *Educational Leadership, 43*(7), 4–11.

Marzane, R. J. (1986). Daisy Arrendando: A framework for teaching thinking. *Educational Leadership, 43*(8), 20–27.

Nickerson, R. (1985). Understanding understanding. *American Journal of Education, 93,* 201–239.

Parker, W. C. (1987). Teaching thinking: The pervasive approach. *Journal of Teacher Education, 37,* 50–56.

Tennyson, R. O., & Cochlarella, M. J. (1986). An empirically based instructional design theory for teaching concepts. *Review of Educational Research, 56,* 40–71.

7

Teaching to an Objective

Teaching to an objective is a process that adds rigor to instruction but does *not* impose rigidity on teaching. It simply means that the actions of teacher and students lead to a desired outcome rather than learning energy being dissipated unintentionally on inconsequential or nonrelevant matters. The process of teaching to an objective ensures that in planning, the teacher anticipates necessary information and productive activities that are relevant to the desired learning and selects those that have the greatest possibility for efficient, successful achievement. This selection is a far cry from covering the material and "hoping" learning will happen. It is the basis for outcome-based education.

More than a quarter of a century ago, Bob Mager focused educators on "behavioral objectives," with a pioneering explanation of the necessity of precision in the content to be learned and the observable student behavior that would validate that learning. As with many good ideas, it became trivialized by zealots into unimportant objectives that were easily measured. The majority of these trivial objectives were set only at the knowledge and comprehension levels of thinking, that is, at lower-level thinking, involving recall and reproduction. We have come a long way in our curricular knowledge since then, and we are now developing objectives that emphasize higher-level thinking, requiring the use of concepts, generalizations, and discriminations. We need to direct our teaching focus on those objectives, selected by teacher and/or students, that have the most transfer potential and are worth students' time and effort.

Objectives do not have to be elaborate. They simply specify what will be learned and students' perceivable behavior to validate that it has been learned. (NOT what the teacher will do.) Examples are:

- The learner will write a one-page summary of the story.
- The learner will solve two-step word problems.
- The learner will contribute ideas to the group discussion.

In contrast, vague, nonobservable outcomes use verbs such as *know, understand, really appreciate,* and *comprehend.*

The *time* and *effort* of students and the teacher are the currency of teaching. That's what we use to achieve learning. We can use it wisely on objectives perceived as valuable by students, or we can fritter it away on inconsequential objectives or on inefficient, and therefore ineffective, teaching and learning behaviors.

Understanding Instructional Objectives

An instructional objective is a statement that makes precise the intended learning and the perceivable student behavior that will validate its achievement. Obviously, our first concern should be the value of the instructional objective to the student. The quality of the student's written message is more important than the slant of the letters. The ability to set up an equation that will solve the problem and then to estimate the accuracy of the answer is more important than lightning speed with number facts. The ability to engage in dialectical thinking (reasonably, responsibly, and respectfully considering an opposing point of view) is more important than memorizing names, dates, and battlegrounds. With valuable and transferable outcomes (objectives) as a given, let's examine the impetus that teaching to an objective gives to successful achievement.

"The student will create an original statement" is an important objective in the arts.

To determine what belongs in a lesson, the teacher needs first to specify in observable terms the specific, desired learning outcome, that is, the instructional objective. Next, the teacher diagnoses students' entry behavior formally, informally, or inferentially (on the basis of knowledge of similar students taught in the past). This behavior establishes the baseline from which students must build learning. Then, a task analysis of the outcome behavior (see chapter 5) identifies the component learnings essential to achieving the objective. Finally, the teacher sequences those learnings that must be acquired in a certain order before the major objective is attainable. This is called a *dependent* sequence since each new learning depends on previous ones having been accomplished (for example, addition of one-digit numbers *before* two-digit numbers with regrouping, *before* three-digit numbers with regrouping).

As discussed earlier, there also is an *independent* sequence, for which it makes no difference which learning is accomplished first. It doesn't matter whether a student learns to subtract single-digit numbers before or after s/he learns to add two-digit numbers, or whether adjectives or adverbs are learned first.

It is task analysis that helps teachers know what learnings (*not* activities or learning styles, which are to be planned later) to include or exclude from each lesson. All learning activities planned for a lesson should lead to the intended observable outcome: the instructional objective.

Some Cautions About Objectives

Using an instructional objective does not mean the teacher can't add humor, include students' interests, attend to students' nonrelevant observations, respond *briefly* to students' nonrelated questions, or *change to a different objective*. However, it does mean that the major part of students' time and effort is directed toward those activities essential to accomplishing the intended learning. The teacher needs to make very rapid, "on your feet" decisions about which student comments or questions are relevant and should be developed and which are nonrelevant and should be briefly acknowledged but not dealt with in depth at the time.

Suppose your objective is, "The learner will write a persuasive essay that incorporates his/her point of view with data to support it, plus presenting evidence that would refute contending points of view." Teaching to that objective would include students' developing a point of view, assembling strong evidence to support it, anticipating contending points of view, gathering objective evidence to refute or dilute those arguments, and expressing all of the above in a coherent, well-stated argument. Activities that are related and important but *not in* that lesson are those that focus on spelling, punctuation, form, neatness, and spacing. Other "bird walks" (digressions intefering with learning) that consume precious time and energy but that would not be appropriate in this lesson (even though they could be very interesting, appropriate, and valuable for a different lesson) are "the reasons people don't agree," "why we should have varying points of view," "there is not always one right answer," or "why direct experience is important."

All of the above are worthy of a lesson designed to accomplish those understandings, but they are teaching to opposite directions, "north by south," in a lesson designed to help students achieve the skill and art of written persuasion. Should any one of them arise in the lesson, however, if the teacher deems it more important or feels "this is the teachable moment" for that learning, the teacher may make the decision to abandon the original objective and teach to the new one: "Students will discuss the value of differing points of view."

It is difficult, however, to design effective instruction with the students in front of you. (It's hard enough to do it in quiet, uninterrupted planning time!) Consequently, often it's a wise teaching decision to make note of the important addition and prepare for its subsequent presen-

No one doubts the presence of an objective when the intended outcome is something to eat!

tation by saying, "That's such an important idea we will come back to it tomorrow and develop it further." This gives the teacher an opportunity to design an artistic and effective lesson for that new outcome and dignifies the student who introduced it.

On the basis of "making the most of students' contributions" and "eliciting students' participation" (both are desirable), some lessons become quagmires of free associations. The following is an example of such a lesson where the objective was, "In preparation for alliterations, the learner will generate words containing the *bl* blend."

Teacher: Today, we're going to learn about words that begin with the *bl* blend. You know what a blend is don't you? You blend things together, like when you bake a cake, you blend the cake mix and the liquid. How many of you have seen someone bake a cake? (Many students raise hands.) "What kind of a cake did the person bake, Tommy?"

Student: Chocolate.

Teacher: Chocolate is most people's favorite. Raise your hand if you like chocolate. Does anyone have a different favorite? What is yours, Charlie?

Student: Coconut.

Teacher: How many like coconut cake?

Student: We don't bake cakes at home. We buy them at the store.

Teacher: Oh, it's done very differently in commercial bakeries. They use 100-pound sacks of flour. They're about this tall and this big around. I couldn't even lift one. Maybe I could if I worked on weight lifting. How many of you have tried to lift weights? (Hands) Well in a bakery, they use hand trucks and dump the flour into a giant bowl. It's big enough to hold you. How would you like to be baked in a cake? (Groans and ahs)

As the lesson continued, the teacher wound up describing assembly lines for cakes (and cars!), with the students wondering "What's going on?" Again, assembly lines are important but not in a lesson on *bl* blends.

Contrast this with a lesson where the objective was the same, but the teacher introduced the *bl* blend with a poem about "blossoms blooming in the blowing wind." Then teacher and students created other alliterative phrases such as "black blouse," "blowing blimp," "blustery blizzard," "blue blazer." Finally, partners developed their own alliterations, using their creativity and a dictionary, and then read them to the class. (This assumes using a dictionary already has been taught.) Teacher freedom and artistry certainly were not lost, but keeping the focus on the *bl* blend, plus excluding nonrelevant activities, contributed to students' success.

In the example of cake baking, the departure from the original objective is obvious. In many cases, it may not be so. A lesson was observed where the objective was, "The learner will summarize a piece of literature." The teacher introduced the lesson by stating the objective and listing several valid reasons why summarizing is an important skill and how that ability speeds up learning and assists retention.

Then the students were assessed to validate that they could state their understanding of the importance of summarizing and the many ways that the skill could assist them throughout life.

Following their statements, the teacher assigned students a piece of literature to read and summarize in writing. At no point in the lesson

Opportunities to manipulate are also important learning objectives.

was a summary defined, or models shown, or the process of separating main ideas and events from inconsequential detail taught. Students had no opportunity to learn the skill or to practice it, with the teacher monitoring their progress to eliminate initial misunderstandings and errors.

While the superficial aspects of the above lesson looked good, clearly the teacher had not taught to the objective of summarizing literature. Instead, the teacher had taught to "The learner will explain why summarizing is an important learning skill." That also is an important objective, but it does not equip students with the skill for subsequently summarizing literature.

Suppose the objective is, "The learners will have the opportunity to hear and enjoy poetry read by the teacher." Which of the following activities belong in the lesson?

1. Students listen to funny poems, poems with descriptive language, and poems with surprise endings.
2. Students listen to a history of the poet's life.
3. Students indicate which poem they liked best.
4. Having heard the poems, students choose those they want to reread.
5. Students subtract the poet's birth date from today's date.
6. Students memorize the poem.
7. Students identify the meter of the poem.

Clearly activities 1, 3, and 4 have greater probability of producing the learning outcome. All of the other activities could be important objectives in subsequent lessons.

Once teachers develop the sophistication of "teaching to the objective" by designing lessons where selected activities will lead with greater probability to the intended learning outcome, students' success becomes more probable and predictable. Again, we reiterate, this does not mean rigidity in teaching but rather rigor in planning, plus decision making *while* teaching. These skills make professional artistry possible, and successful learning probable.

Bibliography

Clark, C. (1988). The necessity for curriculum objectives. *Journal of Curriculum Studies, 20,* 339–349.

Hughes, A. L., & Frommer, K. (1982). A system for monitoring affective objectives. *Educational Leadership, 39,* 521–523.

Mager, R. F. (1962). *Planning objectives for programmed instruction.* Belmont, CA: Fearon Publishers.

Ornstein, A. (1987). Emphasis on student outcomes focuses attention on quality of instruction. *NASSP Bulletin, 71,* 88–95.

Popham, W. J. (1987). Two-plus decades of educational objectives. *International Journal of Educational Research, 11,* 31–41.

8

Planning for Effective Instruction: Lesson Design[1]

Skill in planning is acknowledged to be one of the most influential factors in successful teaching. Should there be a system to this planning or does one hope for a burst of inspiration from which effective instruction automatically will flow? While teacher educators are all for inspiration, we agree with Edison, that well-directed "planning perspiration" *plus* inspiration will work wonders in increasing learners' successful achievement. We believe that a systematic consideration of seven elements, which research

"Planning for Effective Instruction" by Madeline Hunter and Doug Russell. *Instructor*, September 1977. Copyright © 1977 by Scholastic Inc. Reprinted by permission.

has shown to be influential in learning and which therefore should be deliberately *included* or *excluded* in the plan for instruction, will make a great deal of difference in learners' success or lack of it.

It is assumed that *before* a teacher begins to plan for a particular day's teaching, the following decisions, which make effective instruction probable, will have been made:

1.   Within each general content or process area, the teacher will have determined the particular strand for immediate diagnosing and teaching. For example, in the general content area of reading, the teacher might diagnose and teach to either students responding to a piece of literature or identifying main theme or separating fact from opinion or increasing decoding skills. In a process area, the learning could be metacognition, brainstorming, or the generation of meaning in terms of a student's own experience; that is, what the student already knows.

2.   The teacher will have identified a major target objective in the strand and have diagnosed students' achievement in relation to that objective. For example, the teacher will identify students' ability to respond to literature, determine which students can identify main theme, separate fact from opinion, or use beginning consonants to decode words. When a teacher determines which students need to learn a particular content, process, or appreciation, learning opportunities to accomplish that particular objective need to be planned.

3.   On the basis of a diagnosis, the teacher will have selected the specific objective for the total group's or the subgroup's subsequent instruction. ("The learners will write their responses to the story, indicating the feelings it evoked" or "The learners will generate meaning in relation to self" or "The learners will select the main idea and underline it" or "The learners will place an *F* by each statement that is a fact and an *O* by each that is an opinion.")

Only after these three determinations (specific content, students' entry behaviors, target objectives) have been made is the teacher ready to *plan* for tomorrow's learning opportunity—regardless of whether the plan is implemented by direct input from the teacher, by materials, by computer, or by the students themselves in discovery or cooperative learning. Elements in a planning sequence are necessary for *every* mode of learning, not just direct instruction.

For each instructional session, the teacher must consider the following seven elements separately to determine whether or not each element is relevant for the particular content or process objective, for *these* students in *this* situation. Thus, a decision has to be made as to whether that element should be included, excluded, or combined with another element.

There are important nonlanguage ways of making statements that reveal a student's learning. Both language and nonlanguage expressions grow through instruction and practice into creativity.

If the element is included, how to effectively sequence and integrate it into an *artistic* "flow" of instruction is the essence of the planning task. *Teacher decision making is the basis of this approach to teaching.* "Decide, then design" is the foundation on which all successful instruction is built.

When *designing* lessons, the teacher needs to consider the elements in a certain order since each element is derived from and has a relationship to previous elements. Also a decision must be made about inclusion or exclusion of each element in the final design. When the design is *implemented* in teaching, the sequence of the elements included is determined by the professional judgment of the teacher.

1. What Instructional Input Is Needed?

All lesson design begins with articulation of an instructional objective. It specifies the perceivable student behavior that validates achievement of the *precise content or process or skill* that is to be the learning outcome.

To plan the instructional input needed to achieve the target objective, the teacher must determine what information (new or already possessed) the student needs in order to accomplish the intended outcome. Students should not be expected to achieve an objective without having the opportunity to learn that which is essential in order for them to succeed. Task analysis is the process by which the teacher identifies the component learnings or skills essential to the accomplishment of an objective. (See chapter 5.)

Once the necessary information, process, or skill has been identified, the teacher needs to select the means for "getting it in students' heads." Will it be done by discovery, inquiry, teacher presentation, book, film, record, filmstrip, field trip, diagram, picture, real objects, demonstration? Will it be done individually, collaboratively, or in a larger group? The possibilities are legion, and there is no one that is always best.

Examples

- The teacher explains.
- A film is used to give information or demonstrate an activity.
- Students use library resources.
- Students discover the information by doing laboratory experiments or field observations.

In a lesson designed to increase fluency or to develop automaticity, often no input is needed. The input has occurred in previous lessons.

2. What Type of Modeling Will Be Most Effective?

It is facilitating for students not only to know about, but to *see* or *hear*, examples of an acceptable finished product (story, poem, model, diagram, graph) or observe a person's actions or articulated decisions in performing a task (how to identify the main idea, weave, determine ways of thinking or making decisions while fulfilling the assignment).

It is important that the visual input of *modeling* be accompanied by the verbal input of *labeling* the critical elements of what is happening (or has happened) so that students are focused on essentials rather than being distracted by transitory or nonrelevant factors in the process or product.

Examples

- "I am going to use my thumb to work the clay in here like this so the tail has a firm foundation where it is joined to the body of the animal. In that way, it's less likely to break off in the kiln."

- "While I do this problem, I'll tell you what I'm thinking as I work."
- "Notice that this story has a provocative introductory paragraph that catches your interest by the first question the author asks."

In lessons designed to produce divergent thinking or creativity, the teacher usually should not model because students will tend to imitate. The modeling should have occurred in previous lessons so that students have acquired a repertoire of alternatives from which they synthesize an outcome satisfying to them.

3. How Will I Check for Understanding?

The teacher needs to know at what point students possess the information and/or skill necessary to achieve the instructional objective. The following are some ways of ascertaining this.

Sampling
Sampling means posing questions to the total group, allowing them time to think, and then calling on class members representative of strata of the group (most able, average, least able). This process focuses everyone on the generation of an answer and develops student readiness to hear an affirmation or challenge of his/her answer. Note that at the beginning of learning, correct answers are most enabling. Therefore, it is recommended that the teacher at first call on able students to avoid incorrect answers, which can "pollute" learning.

Examples
State the question or give the direction, then give thinking time before naming a student to respond:

- "Be ready to summarize the results of _____."
- "What do you believe were the reasons that Washington was a great leader? I'll give you a minute to think."
- "How would you estimate the answer?"
- "What operation would you use and why?"

Signaled Responses
Each member of the group makes a response, using a signal. For example, students show their selection of the first, second, third, or fourth alternative by showing that number of fingers, put a pencil straight up for "don't call on me for this question," make a c with a hand when examples are correct or an i when incorrect. Math operations, first letters of words,

and punctuation all can be hand-signaled. Nodding or shaking of heads, use of counting sticks, and pointing to a place in the book or to parts in a diagram or to objects are samples of the many signals that can validate learning, or lack of it, for each member of the group.

Examples

- "Nod your head if you agree. Shake your head if you don't."
- "Signal whether you add, subtract, multiply, or divide, by making that sign with your fingers."
- "Show a *c* with your fingers if what I say is correct; an *i* if incorrect. Don't do anything if you're not sure."
- "Raise your hand when you are ready to answer this question."
- "On your microscope, point to _____."

Group Choral Response

After the teacher presents a question to the total group and gives thinking time, the strength of a choral response can indicate the general degree of student accuracy and comfort with the learning. However, this method usually does not give information about individuals.

Individual Private Response

A brief written or whispered-to-teacher response makes students accountable for demonstrating possession of, or progress toward, achievement of the needed information or skills.

Examples

- "Write the names of the three important categories we have discussed and one member of each."
- "Do the first part of this problem on your paper."
- "As I walk around, be ready to tell me your topic and the main idea of your paper."

4. How Will I Design Guided/Monitored Practice?

The beginning stages of learning are critical in the determination of future successful performance. Initial errors can "set" and be difficult to eradicate. Consequently, students' initial attempts in new learning should be carefully monitored and, when necessary, guided so they are accurate and successful. Teachers need to practice with the total group or circulate among students to make sure instruction has "taken" before "turning students loose" to practice independently (with no help available). With teacher guidance, the student needs to perform all (or enough) of the task so that clarification or remediation can occur immediately should it be needed. In that way, the teacher is assured that students will subsequently perform the task correctly without assistance rather than be practicing errors when working by themselves.

5. What Independent Practice Will Cement the Learning?

Once students can perform with a minimal amount of errors, difficulty, or confusion, they are ready to develop fluency, along with increased accuracy, by practicing without the supervision and guidance of the teacher. Only at that point can students be given an assignment to practice the new skill or process with little or no teacher direction.

Teachers, like doctors, are successful only when the student no longer needs them. All teaching has as its purpose to make the student as independent as possible. When lessons are carefully planned, student

Regardless of the teaching model, student success results from careful planning and artistic implementation.

independence becomes much more probable. It is important that in independent work, the student does what already has been practiced rather than some *new*, related, or "inverted" endeavor.

An "inverted" assignment is one where a skill is taught and its reciprocal is practiced. It is as if you taught a child how to untie shoes and take them off and then assigned the practice of putting them on and tying them, or you taught addition and then assigned a practice sheet of subtraction. The same situation is created by teaching students to solve word problems and then asking them to generate word problems, teaching punctuation of written sentences and assigning creation of sentences requiring that punctuation, teaching how to recognize a topic sentence and then requiring generation of topic sentences.

6. Should the Students Be Made Aware of the Objective and Its Value?

This element of an effective lesson involves communicating to students what they will learn during the instruction and why that accomplishment is important, useful, and relevant to their present and/or future life situations. It is *not* the pedantic, "At the end of today's lesson you will be able to _____."

Examples

- "You were slowed down yesterday because you had trouble with _____. Today we are going to practice in order that you develop more speed and accuracy."

- "We are going to work on the correct form of letter writing so that you can write for the materials you need in your social studies project."

- "Today you are going to practice ways of participating in a discussion so each of you gets turns and you also learn from other people's ideas."

- "You are going to be surprised to find out what happened after Columbus returned and the difference his voyage made to ways of thinking."

Note that the objective *as stated to the student* is not as it is stated in the teacher's plan book: "The learner will use correct form in writing a letter"; "The learner will list the results of Columbus voyage and explain their significance."

Usually, students will learn more efficiently if they know what the learning will be and why it is important in their lives. There are times, however, when the objective should *not* be known because it will distract them or turn them off. ("Today you are going to learn the difference between colons and semicolons" could elicit "Who cares?")

7. What Anticipatory Set Will Focus Students on the Objective?

"Anticipatory set" results from a *brief* activity that occurs at the beginning of the lesson or when students are mentally "shifting" gears from one activity to the next. The purpose of an anticipatory set is to elicit students' attending behavior, focus them on the content of the ensuing instruction, and develop a mental readiness (or "set") for it. The "set" may (but doesn't need to) include a review of previous learning if it will *help the student achieve today's objective*, but not routine review of old material. The set also may give the teacher some diagnostic data needed for teaching the current objective.

An anticipatory activity should continue only long enough to get students "ready, set to go," so that the major portion of instructional time is available for the accomplishment of the current objective.

Examples
Examples of activities that produce anticipatory set are having students—

- Give synonyms for overused words, when the current objective is improvement in descriptive writing
- Create word problems to go with a numeral problem on the chalkboard, when the current objective is meaningful computation practice
- Review the main ideas of yesterday's lesson, which will be extended today
- State ways a skill might be useful in daily life, when the objective is to develop fluency with that skill
- Practice speedy answers to multiplication facts for a quick review before today's math lesson on two-place multiplication

An anticipatory set is *not* needed if students are already alert and "ready to go" because yesterday's teaching built a bridge or transition to today's lesson.

Summary

Not all the seven elements just described will be included in every lesson. It may take several lessons before students are ready for guided and/or independent practice. Also, *mere presence of an element in a lesson does not guarantee quality teaching*. A teacher may use an anticipatory set that spreads rather than focuses students' attention ("Think of your favorite food; today we are going to talk about cereals"). Input may be done ineffectively. The modeling may be distracting ("I will cut this chocolate cupcake in fourths"). The seven elements are guides in *planning* for creative and effective lessons. They are not mandates!

Simply "knowing" the seven elements of planning for effective instruction will not ensure that those elements are implemented effectively. Also, simply having a "knack with kids" will not ensure the elements that promote successful learning will be included in instructional planning. Both the science and the art of teaching are essential. It is the belief of the writer, however, that deliberate consideration of these seven elements, which can promote effective instruction, constitutes the launching pad for planning effective and artistic teaching (using *any* model of teaching with *any* type of student) to achieve greater student achievement of *any* objective or goal.

Bibliography

Brown, D. S. (1988). Twelve middle-school teachers planning. *The Elementary School Journal, 89*(1), 69–87.

Condon, D., & Maggs, A. (1986). Direct instruction research: An international focus. *International Journal of Special Education, 1,* 35–47.

Doyle, W. (1984). *Effective classroom practices for secondary schools.* R & D Report No. 6191. Austin: Texas University Research and Development Center for Teacher Education.

Gagné, E. D. (1985). Strategies for effective teaching and learning. In *The cognitive psychology of school learning.* Boston: Little, Brown.

Gagné, R. M., & Briggs, L. J. (1974). *Principles of instructional design.* New York: Holt, Rinehart & Winston.

Gerston, R. (1986). Direct instruction: A research-based approach to curriculum design and teaching. *Exceptional Children, 53,* 17–31.

Kallison, J. M. (1986). Effects of lesson organization on achievement. *American Educational Research Journal, 23*(2), 337–347.

Moore, J. (1986). Direct instruction: A model of instructional design. *Educational Psychology, 6,* 201–229.

Pratton, J., & Hates, L. W. (1985). The effects of active participation on student learning. *Journal of Educational Research, 79,* 210–215.

Rosenshine, B., & Stevens, R. (1986). Teaching functions. In M. C. Wittrock (Ed.), *Handbook of Research on Training* (3rd ed., pp. 375–391). New York: Macmillan.

Section

3

Decisions
About
Learning
Behaviors

Teachers are working with the most complex
thing that exists in the universe: the human brain.
Yet, until the last half of this century, very little
was known about how the brain functioned. We
still are only at the "tip of the iceberg" with our
knowledge of brain functioning; a great deal of
the complexity of the brain remains to be dis-

covered. Now, however, we have enough important information about how the brain "works" to
guide decisions about learning behaviors and the
necessity that each student's brain generate
meaning to achieve learning (relating what is
already known to what is being learned). While
the skilled teacher can facilitate generation of
meaning, this task must be done by the student if
comprehension is to occur.

The first chapter in this section, chapter 9,
summarizes, in "teaching language," information learned from psychoneurology that is useful in instruction.

Chapter 10 discusses implications for teaching from the studies of hemispheric specializa-
tion of the brain, that is, left hemispheric vs. right
hemispheric processing. The focus is on how the
information can be used to affect students' learning behaviors, without elaborate testing. A major
educational objective is to increase the modalities
with which students are facile rather than lim-
iting them to a few comfortable ones, which the
environment may not always accommodate.
Students will need to use all modalities in order
to function efficiently in the modern world, and
teachers need to introduce activities to stimulate
both the left hemisphere and the right hemisphere
and help students build proficiency with both
hemispheres.

Chapter 11 translates the knowledge of the
brain's functioning into specific principles for
the most effective use of a chalkboard, overhead,
or any other visual input system, always with the
objective of enhancing student achievement. "Oh,
I *see* what you mean!" can become reality.

Chapter 12 deals with the powerful effects
of observational learning. By observing, we can
imitate behaviors; in fact, most of our speech patterns and gestures and many of our beliefs, values, and actions result from observation. When
you place a student in charge of your class, you

can often watch yourself teach. The student had no "motivation" or intent to learn your ways. The student's imitative behavior came from observational learning. The results alert us to how much can be learned through observation, with the learner being unaware that learning is occurring. Teachers need to be able to use students' imitative power productively rather than by happenstance and to deliberately incorporate observational learning from appropriate models in planning for instruction.

9

Research on the Brain as a Basis for Teaching Decisions

We have learned more about the human brain and how it functions in the last two decades than we had learned from the beginning of time. Even with this explosion of information, we have only scratched the surface of knowledge about the brain—the most complex thing that exists in the universe. The current questions are, "Does the brain have the capacity to understand itself? If it does, can it use what it understands to help itself function with constantly increasing effectiveness?"

Much of neuropsychology or psychoneurology (the fields are becoming so entwined that it is becoming difficult to tell one from the other) is still at a level that translation of research into

103

suggestions for increasingly effective teaching is difficult and some-times impossible. Yet, we can intelligently extrapolate from some of the findings to determine what educators might do more effectively "tomor-row morning."

Sensations and Perceptions

Sensations (neural stimuli) that impinge on our receptors (eyes, nose, mouth, skin, muscles, and so on) are transmitted through neural pathways to our brain's sensory register (the brain's intake mechanism), where those sensations are translated into perceptions (imbued with meaning) or they fade (decay). For example, did you hear an airplane today? If one flew overhead, the sound waves hit your ears, but you may have "paid no attention" to it and the sensory trace faded without your con-scious identification that it had occurred. On the other hand, if you were on your way to the airport to meet a friend, you probably "heard" the plane and wondered if it were the one on which your friend was arriving.

Assigning meaning to a sensation creates a *perception* in short-term memory. A perception involves matching the information in your sensory register with a pattern in long-term memory (your memory stor-age bin). You remember how an airplane sounds, and the current audi-tory sensation matches that memory. After identifying the sound, you may discard the perception as unimportant and later may not even "remember" you heard it. The perception of hearing an airplane was not encoded into long-term memory and consequently was not avail-able for later retrieval. You "forgot it."

On the other hand, if the perception was encoded into long-term memory, you may "remember" that you heard your friend's plane as it was arriving and be able to reactivate that memory at a later date.

All of this comes as no surprise to any teacher who knows that some students never "hear" what they are told. Some students hear it, can repeat it, but can't "remember" it later. Other students hear it and can remember it for future recall and use.

Increasing "Paying Attention"

Obviously, we wish to increase the probability of students' remembering, so we need to use what we know about how the brain functions to achieve students' "paying attention" (creating perceptions), learning (processing in working memory, that is, thinking about it), and "remem-bering" (storing information in long-term memory and retrieving it when needed).

The brain "pays attention" to something that is perceived as important. It is assumed (no one really knows) that what is important was linked originally to survival. Consequently, certain characteristics of sensations have potential for eliciting attention or the "alerting reflex." You can see physical evidence of this alerting reflex in the behavior of dogs or cats who appear to be snoozing. Suddenly they lift their heads, their ears go up, and they stare in a certain direction. You can also see it in an electroencephalogram as a "spiking" of the brain waves. That means the organism is "paying attention," or focusing on something that has entered the sensory register.

If, in the matching of that sensation to a pattern in the organism's long-term memory, the perception is interpreted as unimportant or non-relevant, the sensation decays (ceases to exist), the brain waves go back to normal and the dog or cat goes back to sleep.

If the stimulus is interpreted as something to which attention should continue to be directed (for example, food or danger), the dog or cat may walk in the direction of the sight or sound and do something about it.

A person will process a perception perceived as important from short-term memory to "working memory": the activation and processing in the brain that involves thinking.

An analogy might be thinking of the brain as a switchboard. The phone rings, but you pay no attention. The sound waves hit your ears, but you don't respond and so the caller hangs up (the stimulus decays in the perceptual register). Again, the phone rings, you answer, and the caller says, "May I speak to John Jones?" You respond "You have the wrong number" and hang up. You have changed the sensation to a perception: somebody wants John Jones. You do not see that as relevant to you, so you discard that perception (you don't think about it). A third time, the phone rings, you answer, recognize the voice, and you and a friend have a meaningful conversation. You are processing your perceptions, assigning significance to them, possibly activating related information from long-term memory, and synthesizing meaning in your working memory. You have activated communication. (You are processing information in working memory.)

What is happening in the brain when you are processing information in working memory? Neurons are activated through synoptic firings from axons to dendrites so that brain cells "communicate" with each other. Nothing is actually "moving" in the brain. The activation of neurons underlies the mental process involved in recognizing, recalling, interpreting, and thinking.

Four characteristics of sensations in our sensory registers have high probability of eliciting our alerting reflexes. In classrooms, teachers can use these characteristics to increase the probability of students' "paying attention."

1. Self. The brain cannot ignore important things related to it. We guarantee that as you pass the superintendent's closed door, if you hear your name from inside your ears will "prick up."

Consequently, we increase students' attention and cerebral processing when we use students' names in our classroom examples and relate those examples to students' own lives.

Examples

- "What decision that affects you would you like to have made by majority vote, and why do you think that a majority vote would be a good method?"

- "If our class earned 50 dollars in a car wash, and we decided to bank it for 6 months at 6% interest, how much money would we have for our party?"

- "Let's see how many adjectives you can think of to describe your favorite food."

A student's receptive "screen" signals, "This is about me; therefore, it's important, so I'm going to listen to it and think about it" (process it in working memory).

There is very little we teach in school that we can't relate to the students themselves. Then, as they imbue the concept or generalization with meaning by connecting it with themselves, they are more able to apply it, subsequently, to new situations.

2. Emotion. We suspect the factor of emotion also was related to survival, when early humans "paid attention" to things that were pleasant so they could be repeated and to things that were unpleasant so they could be avoided.

Which sentence would gain more attention from you, "A boy sat in the car" or "A murderer sat in the car"? Obviously, we pay attention to stimuli with emotional loading.

A word of caution needs to be sounded. A student's attention needs to be directed to what is to be learned, rather than distracted by emotion. Consequently, we use emotion only to direct attention to what should be perceived as important. If students are focused on the emotion rather than on the important concept or generalization, emotion has been misused and will interfere with learning. In the example above, if there had recently had been a murder in the news, students' attention could be diverted to that event rather than to the grammar the sentence was designed to illustrate.

3. Discrepant Event. Anything that is different from what we expect or what "should be" elicits the alerting reflex. If on a calm, windless day, the leaves on a nearby bush began moving, early humans knew that they had better pay attention to what was causing the movement.

Something different or unexpected elicits students' attention.

Teachers achieve the same effect by encouraging students to respond to "something different." Underlining, italicizing, different colors or print—all call attention to something we wish students to notice. Standing in a different place in the room, a change of voice, a new procedure, dinosaurs, and mysteries elicit the alerting reflex.

So if students are not "paying attention," you might introduce something novel. Don't make it so different, however, that the students are distracted rather than focused by the difference.

4. *Mands.* You, no doubt, are paying attention to the word *mands*. It may be a word new to you. There's a certain emotion connected to words if you're not sure of their meaning, and it's certainly a discrepant event when sophisticated educators meet a word they don't know.

Let's connect *mand* to a pattern you already have in your long-term memory. It's the same root word you find in *demand, command, mandate,* and *mandatory.* It means something you should do. Your visual sensation from the print on this page has now become a perception in short-term memory, attaining meaning as a result of processing information from long-term memory to working memory, that is, information in long-term memory about other words that contain "mand."

Teachers give a nonverbal mand when they point, underline, demonstrate, or change the tone, juncture (pauses between words), or loudness of their voices. Teachers give a verbal mand when they say, "Now listen carefully!" "Pay attention!" "Notice this!"

Teachers combine alerting stimuli when they say, "Now listen carefully (mand) because you (self) may find this next item on your final exam (emotion)" or "You (self) will learn (mand) about something you never even knew existed (discrepant event)."

For those of you who know motivation theory, you'll find a remarkable similarity to the factors a teacher can alter to increase students' motivation. Interest is aroused by relation to self and novelty (discrepant event). Feeling tone and level of concern are related to emotions and mands. Frequently, researched-based, psychological generalizations are interrelated and have significance in all types of learning.

Storage and Retrieval From Long-Term Memory

Current research suggests that working memory can process seven (plus or minus two) "chunks" of information at one time. A chunk may be a single word or number (Columbus, 9). It can be a concept or pattern ("explorers"—a concept that includes many explorers' names—or the counting pattern of 8, 9, 10). A "chunk" also can be a generalization that previously has been learned ("Explorers seek information new to them and that seeking is approved by their society").

Knowing the typical limitations of working memory causes us to rethink assignments that require working on several new "chunks" at one time (20 spelling words, 25 definitions, the 10 causes of _____). Practice theory, for years, has suggested working on "a short, meaningful part for a short, intense time." In cognitive psychology, the term for mental practice is *rehearsal*.

Rote or Maintenance Rehearsal

Once a perception is in working memory, we need to develop teaching techniques that increase the probability it will remain there long enough to be processed into long-term memory rather than fade (decay). To keep the perception active, we may need to do *rote or maintenance rehearsal* (practice). Have you ever looked up a phone number and then walked to another room to make the call? What do you typically do while you're walking? You say (rehearse) the number over and over to keep it from fading. If someone asks you a question, you shake your head and ignore the question. You know that if you answer the question, you will "forget" the number. It will fade. Rote or identical rehearsal preserves the memory trace in working memory until it can be processed into long-term memory or, if it no longer is necessary (you conclude the phone call), it can be "forgotten."

The brain is the "meaning maker" regardless of the source of information.

After you have made the call, you no longer attempt to remember the number. Remembering involves the storage of information in long-term memory and its retrieval from long-term memory. The words *storage* and *retrieval* imply changing position in space. You will recall from our switchboard example that things don't "move around" in the brain: they are chemically and electrically encoded and activated.

Elaborative Rehearsal of Information

A second and more powerful kind of rehearsal can be achieved by the brain's elaborating on, or adding to, what is being learned. Students generate their own meaning for, or relationships to, what is being learned. To strengthen processing into and retrieval from long-term memory and to reduce the necessity for so much rehearsal (practice), we can encourage students to use five elaboration strategies that require deep processing: the generation of additional meaning as a result of the student making connections with other information in the brain rather than just rote rehearsal. Here are descriptions of these five elaborative processes.

1. Imaging. To image is to activate a previously experienced sensory image from our long-term memories. Imaging is different from imagining, which is creating something we have not experienced. An image from long-term memory can be visual, tactile, auditory, gustatory, olfactory, or a combination of these. To experience for yourself the power of imaging, visualize a very large, ripe, juicy lemon cut in half with the droplets of juice oozing out. Do you "see" it? Now lick it with your tongue. Most of you will experience a flow of saliva in your mouths. Rather than the stimulus coming from the outside world, it comes from a "memory" in the brain. Reality truly does exist in your brain.

When we want to "remember" something, it helps to image it: to see if you can feel, see, smell, taste, hear it in your brain. Athletes and musicians have been "practicing" this way for many years. Imaging is one powerful way to rehearse anything you wish to store or automate for high-speed retrieval from long-term memory.

Some students image much more easily than others. Some image more readily with their eyes closed. Others prefer to keep their eyes open. All of us can improve our ability to image with practice. You, no doubt, have experienced remembering where something was on a page even if you could not recall the exact words or the details.

Imaging (activating the sensory stimulus in long-term memory) is becoming an effective, increasingly routine, rehearsal (practice) activity in learning. The more you practice imaging, the more proficient you become.

2. Paraphrasing. Another powerful way to store information and increase the probability of remembering it is by paraphrasing. Saying the same thing in different words requires activation of synonyms, which is another way of "deep processing." In paraphrasing, the learner accesses information stored in long-term memory that matches the pattern in working memory and then connects meaning with the words in working memory. Paraphrasing brings together what is being thought about or being learned with something already in the brain, and those connections make storage and later retrieval more probable. (Note: Nothing is "certain" with human learning. We are using what we have learned from research to increase probabilities.)

To experience the neural effort (deep processing) required by paraphrasing, try explaining in your own words (not a memorized definition or a synonym) the meaning of *courage, perseverance, amphibian, factoring.* An excellent test of a student's comprehension is to request,

"Say it in your own words." Successful accomplishment usually will result in longer remembering and easier recall.

3. *Summarizing.* A third way to increase the probability of more effective storage and retrieval of information is to create a summary: a distillation of the most important aspects of that information.

To summarize requires identification of the most important aspects, thereby allowing the insignificant to fade or decay. Summarizing requires selective attention to what is perceived as essential rather than cluttering memory with trivia. Developing a shorter form (summary) that includes important aspects and excludes unimportant ones necessitates analytic processing in working memory, which, while requiring considerable neural energy, makes storage and retrieval more efficient and probable.

4. *Examples.* When the learner generates an example from his/her own life knowledge or experience, s/he is identifying a pattern from long-term memory that is similar to the new learning, thereby transferring what is already known to accelerate the acquisition of what is becoming known. The ability to provide a valid example is a certification that a learner has generated meaning. In addition, the example builds connections between the pattern of what is currently being processed and a pattern that already exists in long-term memory. This provides a "glue" that helps builds the connections that prevent fading or forgetting.

An example of the meaning of courage might be, "I was scared to give my report in front of the class but I made myself volunteer to be the first one to do it. That took courage!"

An example of when to use the operation of division might be, "I wanted to be fair and give each of my friends the same amount of time to play with my new video game, so I divided the time we had by the number of friends to find out how much time each should have."

To "prime the student's pump," it is helpful for the teacher to provide examples that have high probability of already being in students' long-term memories and then encourage (require) students to generate their own examples so they are custom-tailored to each student's retrieval process.

5. *Visual Display.* Often a right hemispheric output (that is, a visual display or model) will validate understanding and constitute an elaboration of the concept, generalization, or information being learned. Diagrams, outlines, webs, pictures, and time lines are "right hemispheric," nonverbal examples of the relationships or "connections" that exist or are being constructed in the brain.

Young students can make a picture of the beginning, middle, and end of the story. They can visually depict the "problem" and the "solution." Older students can use pictures, diagrams, graphs, outlines, or webs to show the connections in information visually. This evidence of understanding is particularly important for those students who are not so facile with verbal (oral or writing) skills.

Developing Automaticity

Learning something new takes a great deal of neural energy. As a particular learning (memory) continues to be retrieved (activated), the neural pathways in the brain require less chemical and electrical energy. Eventually, that memory or process can become so automatic it requires very little neural energy for the synaptic firing (connections from axons to dendrites) to occur. This automaticity releases energy for cognitive processing that has not become automatic (problem solving, creativity, new learning).

An analogy might be making a path through a jungle. The first time you go through the jungle all your energy is required to separate the vines and brush. You have no energy to do other things. As you continue to use that route, you form a pathway and eventually you can walk through it, paying very little attention to the path. Your energy is released to use in other ways. Once that path is made, just an occasional walk down it will stamp down any weeds that have grown. We mass practice on new material for fast learning (make the path) and distribute practice for long remembering (occasionally use it to keep the weeds down).

If you were teaching a five-year-old to tie his/her shoes, s/he could not do anything else. It would take all his/her neural energy. You and I can be in a hot political argument and if you notice your shoe is untied, you will tie it while you continue to make your point. Tying your shoe has become automatic. It requires very little neural energy, leaving most of your energy available for engaging in the argument. This is why we do not introduce several new things to students at the same time.

Organization of Information

Finally, it is important that students "file" information in a way that it can be retrieved on cue. In the same way that it is easier for you to locate information in your files if you have a well-organized system, it is easier for students to retrieve "folders" of information rather than separate "pieces." Consequently, information is more easily learned and remembered if relationships among ideas are established. Whether "advance organizers" (file folders) are provided for the student by the teacher, or each student sets up an individual filing system depends on the probability of success. If students can organize information on their own with reasonable success, they should do so because the practice can transfer into their organizing subsequent information. Better the teacher provide the organizers, however, than have unable students work with a mish-mash of material that is not retrievable because it is in nonrelated bits and pieces.

Summary

Knowledge of brain functioning makes it even more important that the teacher be an informed decision maker rather than a robotic, "direction follower." There are no absolutes in teaching and learning. Education is a relativistic, situational profession, based on science plus intuition and creative implementation. Educators, as all professionals, must continue to grow by incorporating new, research-based knowledge on the brain into artistic performances in the classroom, thereby increasing the probability of enabling *all* learners to become increasingly successful.

Bibliography

Anderson, J. (1985). *Cognitive psychology and its implications*. New York: W. H. Freeman.

Ellis, H. C., & Hunt, R. R. (1989). *Fundamentals of human memory and cognition*. Dubuque, IA: William Brown.

Gagné, E. D. (1985). *The cognitive psychology of school learning*. Boston: Little, Brown.

Glover, J., Ronning, R., & Bruning, R. (1990). *Cognitive psychology for teachers*. New York: Macmillan.

Wittrock, M. C. (1974). Learning as a generative process. *Educational Psychologist, 11*, 87–95.

Wittrock, M. C. (1975). Generative processes of comprehension. *Educational Psychology, 24*, 345–376.

Wittrock, M. C. (Ed.) (1986). *Handbook of research on teaching* (3rd ed.). New York: Macmillan.

Wittrock, M. C., & Carter, J. E. (1975). Generative processing of hierarchically organized words. *American Journal of Psychology, 88*, 489–501.

Wittrock, M. C., Doctorow, M. J., & Marks, C. B. (1975). Reading as a generative process. *Journal of Educational Psychology, 67*, 484–489.

Wittrock, M. C., & Goldberg, S. M. (1975). Imagery and meaningfulness in free recall: Word attributes and instructional sets. *Journal of General Psychology, 92*, 137–151.

Yarmen, A. D., & Brown, N. V. (1972). The role of imagery in incidental learning of educable retarded and normal children. *Journal of Experimental Child Psychology, 14*, 303–312.

10

Sense (and Non-sense)
About Your Students'
Right and Left
Hemispheres

"Why should I read the directions? I can *see* how it goes together." This obviously correct observation has baffled many a teacher as a student confidently confronted a bewildering array of pieces. And s/he *could* see how it went together while his/her seemingly more able classmates struggled through decoding "attach narrow end of part A to rounded side of part B" in order to ferret out the knowledge that would guide their actions.

That same puzzling student would protest, "Don't tell me how to get there, draw me a map," while his/her bewildered teacher pleads, "Don't show me a map, just *tell* me how to get there."

Teacher and student scratched their heads as each wondered how the other ever survived in this complex world. Each acknowledged the other seemed to have good results, but "it's beyond me how s/he thinks."

Such differences in thinking and remembering ("I don't remember what s/he said but I can describe the room we were in" vs. "I don't remember where it was but I can tell you what s/he said," or "Let's lay it out on paper" vs. "Let's talk about it") generate different ways of attacking problems. Different styles of learning have been dealt with in the past by dumping those variations in the "people are different" basket. Now research into the functioning of hemispheres of the brain has begun to sort that basket into the categories of left- and right-brained thinking,[1] with promising and productive suggestions for teachers that could accelerate the learning outcomes of all students.

Like Ponce de Leon searching for the fountain of youth, educators have continued to seek a fountain of eternal literacy where immersion in some new program or technique will solve all the problems of student learning. The flood of information from research into the brain, publicizing the difference in functions of human's right and left hemispheres, is seen by many as a promising pathway to this elusive elixir. International interest, investigation, and a great deal of sense and "nonsense" are the result.

The Functions of the Two Hemispheres

Research in hemisphericity indicates that humans have two hemispheres in the brain, each complete in itself. Unlike animals, humans begin, at an early age, to differentiate the data processed by each hemisphere. While many things are processed in both hemispheres, in most people the left hemisphere "specializes" in information where significance is based in relationships that are built across time. Most of you are using your left hemisphere as you relate what you are now reading to what you read in the previous paragraph and what you will read in the next paragraph. The left hemisphere has been called the *temporal* or *propositional*, "if-then" brain because relationships are processed analytically and across time.

The right hemisphere in most humans "specializes" in data where significance emerges from relationships that must be perceived across space. You are using your right hemisphere when, from the surrounding visual environment, you are aware of where you are in the building, recognize a face, or understand data displayed on a chart, graph, or

---

[1]While most neurologists agree that there is *one* brain (there are some dissenters), the expression "right-brained" is often used instead of "right hemispheric" and "left-brained" instead of "left hemispheric."

diagram. The right hemisphere has been called the *visual-spatial* or *appositional* brain.

The right and left hemispheres are connected by an impressive bundle of nerve fibers, the corpus callosum, which transmits messages from one hemisphere to the other to produce "integrated brain thinking." Consequently, while the stimulus or input to each hemisphere may be planned (for example, speech for the left hemisphere, diagrams for the right), the individual's processing of perceptions cannot be controlled from the outside because either hemisphere may communicate with the other for an "assist." Thus, the individual may attach internal words to an external diagram or, conversely, construct an internal diagram to match the words being read or heard.

A somewhat similar analogy is that we have "assigned" certain responsibilities to our hands (holding the book with our left hand while we point to the word or turn the page with our right hand, cutting with our right hand while we manipulate the material with the left). No matter how able we are with our right hand, we do most things more efficiently and effectively if we also use our left hand. In like manner, integrated brained thinking occurs when each hemisphere augments the information processed by the other.

Music, for example, is usually considered a right hemisphere function. A simple melody may be processed and recognized in the right hemisphere by a nonmusician. A musician, however, may process the same auditory stimulus differently, analyzing the harmony, tonal patterns, theme variations, and so on, in the left hemisphere. Our language reflects this dual processing as we say, "Yes, I understand" or "Oh, I see" or "I see what you are saying."

The Hemispheres and Teaching

Increased knowledge and understanding of brain functioning have generated a great many simplistic (and often spurious) solutions to some of the most complex problems in human functioning: "normal learning," "learning disability," or "minimal brain dysfunction" (M.B.D.). One well-meaning but misinformed superintendent of schools employed a number of music teachers to stimulate students' right hemispheres, hoping thereby to increase their reading scores. In some cases, students are instructed to cover one eye so that the functioning of the opposite brain hemisphere will be stimulated. Classroom meditation is being scheduled, cult religions are in vogue, and a myriad of virtues (creativity, feelings, intuition, and so on) are being attributed to the formerly less publicized right hemisphere. At this point of knowledge, the truth of the matter can be stated:

- Reading or any other content test scores will respond most positively to increased skill in the teaching of that content.
- From each eye, the optic nerve splits and goes to both hemispheres.
- While religion and meditation have virtues of their own, they do not seem to be the panacea for learning problems.
- The potential for creativity emerges from each hemisphere: both an elegant theory and a Taj Mahal are creative products.
- Feelings emerge from the limbic regions of the brain (midbrain), not from the hemispheres.
- While intuition is often an interpretation of the right hemisphere's visual or sound perceptions ("She *looks* as if she doesn't mean what she says" or "He *sounds* as if he doesn't mean what he says"), the interpretation of those sights and sounds ("Therefore, he or she must really mean . . . and I had better") often needs a logical assist from the left hemisphere before that "intuitive" judgment is completed.

Clearly, we are only on the periphery of understanding the functioning of the human brain. Present knowledge, however, gives us many defensible and potentially effective suggestions that can be incorporated in teaching so that we can make students' learning more predictably successful.

Genetic Predisposition vs. Practice

While an individual may have genetic predisposition to facility with analytic, sequential (left hemisphere) or visual-spatial, simultaneous (right hemisphere) processing, there is no doubt that much of any individual's preference and facility can result from practice.

Researchers suspect that an individual may be born with a predisposition to prefer, or find it easier to use, his/her right or left hemisphere; however, as with right- or left-handedness, it is known that practice has a great deal to do with skill. (Witness the right-handed pianist who plays beautifully with his/her left hand, the typist who makes no more errors with his/her left hand than with the right hand, or the artisan who needs both hands and so uses them both with almost equal dexterity.) Without practice, skills and processes can become stagnant so that the comfort of using the dominant hand (or hemisphere) often results in the subordinate hand (or hemisphere) getting minimal use. As a result, the lack of skill that results from too little practice is often incorrectly interpreted as lack of inherent ability.

Much of facility is situational. The insensitive business executive who doesn't "know" the feelings (see their nonverbal signals?) of his/her associates may know (see?) the minute on entering the door that his/her spouse is in a "mood" and s/he had better tread softly. Some researchers can thread their way through a labyrinth of the most complicated if-then elaborations but can't follow the "directions on the can." The teacher who doesn't notice what Johnny wears can tell at the first glance that it's going to be one of "those days" with him. Testing for recruits that were gifted in mechanical and spatial relationships, the army found that young men who grew up on farms were by far the majority in the population identified. These young men had spent many hours tinkering with tractors, repairing things, plowing fields, loading trucks, and so on. Who knows the part contributed by heredity or by experience to their "giftedness"?

Previous experience also seems to be true of "brainedness." Because a student can "see" how it goes together, s/he uses his/her more facile right-hemisphere and may not give his/her left the practice of reading and following directions. Because other students can get their instructions more easily from reading, they don't practice "seeing" if they can figure it out without the words.

The assumption that native ability is extended or diminished by practice is supported by current research that indicates that *measured* I.Q.

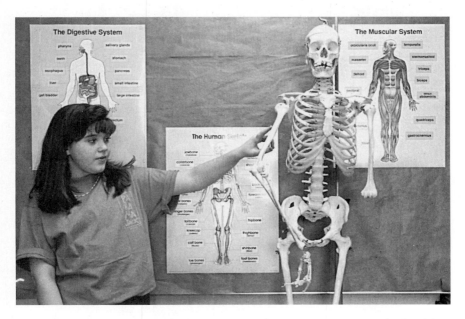

Learners need both right and left hemispheric input so they become facile with both.

can change with prescribed changes in experience. In no way, however, should these statements be construed as indicating that all difference in human performance is the result of experience. We still can't make every learner equal. There *are* genetic differences.

Educators and brain researchers are becoming suspicious that the boy who knew everything about a carburetor, but couldn't read the test on carburetion systems or couldn't write the answers that he had already demonstrated in action that he knew, or the girl who did well in algebra, but almost flunked geometry, could be (not necessarily are) victims of our lack of understanding of hemisphericity. We are beginning to suspect that the student who can't remember what s/he heard in the story, but can describe in detail a television program, and the one who is confused by the diagram, but can sequence perfectly the story s/he read, are mirror images of the same phenomenon. In like manner, the student who can say the words in the book, but doesn't comprehend what has been read, or

Building visual representations gives a right-hemispheric assist to left-hemispheric generalizations.

the student to whom the graph is a mystery, may represent *our* deficit in understanding rather than theirs.

For educators, this suggests that, rather than wasting time in elaborate testing to identify a student's preferred mode of hemispheric processing, we should provide students with many opportunities to use both. Sequential (left hemisphere) and simultaneous (right hemisphere) processing should be provided both separately and in tandem so a repertoire of learning strategies can be acquired by the student. Just as students accomplish more work if they use both hands, they'll probably accomplish more learning when they use both hemispheres.

Implications for Classroom Practice

Now what do all of these interesting findings mean to educators in the conduct of day-to-day schooling? First, they clearly mandate the responsibility for conducting instruction so that, whenever possible, information that is presented in a linear fashion across time (reading it or hearing it) is also presented in visual space (seeing or imaging it) so that students have practice in integrating the information from their two hemispheres. Second, these findings suggest that whenever a student is not "getting it," the stimulus should be augmented or replaced with one that is aimed at the other hemisphere. Third, deliberate incorporation of practice that could increase facility in the use of each hemisphere separately and in concert with the other should become an important educational objective.

Rather than elaborate diagnostic schemes to determine which hemisphere a learner prefers, instruction to achieve this integrated processing would include these elements:

1. Presenting material that is aimed at each of the two hemispheres simultaneously
2. Augmenting a stimulus to one hemisphere by following it with information beamed to the opposite hemisphere
3. Deliberate beaming to only one hemisphere for practice to increase fluency in processing one type of information
4. Using examples from the student's own life or experience to elicit imaging (seeing and feeling what is meant)

Let's look at examples of each of the above professional strategies in turn.

1. Presenting Material to Both Hemispheres. Schools long have realized the importance of augmenting the written or spoken word with chalkboard, pictures, diagrams, graphs, and so on. As technology advances, more sophisticated audio (left-brained) and visual (right-brained) materials have become available to teachers.

The audio of spoken words (not music), while using the same language (left-brained) input system as reading, eliminates the barrier created by the need to possess the skill of decoding letter symbols into meaning. Without knowing the neurological reason, we knew visuals were important. Unfortunately, however, "audiovisual" became an end in itself, with millions of dollars being spent on materials that in some cases were poorly designed, ineffectively executed, and unintelligently used.

With the advent of television, which is primarily a right-brained input system (configurations of dots in space to which significance is assigned) and which is augmented by the temporal input of speech (often the same few words repeated over and over as in TV commercials), the whole world, literate and illiterate, is able to receive information without so much left-brained processing, surmounting the hurdle of having to decode written words into meaning. With television, the right-brained individual can take his/her proper "place in the sun" with his/her left-brained, formerly advantaged friends, in terms of knowing about and understanding both current and past issues. Human artistic achievement or even the horrors of disasters are no longer privileged communications limited to the "ones who were there" or the left-brained scholars.

While language and linguistic markers are processed in the left hemisphere, it is interesting to note that the clues of timbre, intonation, pitch, and so on, in spoken words are processed in the right hemisphere (as is music). "Hearing what s/he says" and "hearing what s/he means" can be different messages, each processed in a different hemisphere and posing the problem as to which message the receiver accepts as the valid one. Recently, nonverbal communication—the interpretation of kinetic (movement), iconic (images), and sonorous (sound) clues—has come into high visibility as a right hemisphere function. "Intuition" could be a manifestation of this kind of "knowing" without being told by words.

It is important for the teacher to note that his/her own verbal and nonverbal communication must deliver the same message or "what you do speaks so loudly I can't hear what you say" may result. The younger child is particularly responsive to nonverbal cues. For integrated perception and development of facility with both hemispheres, language plus visual and kinetic plus sonorous clues constitute the most effective communicative process. Our expression and movements must match our words.

Modeling often is an effective way to simultaneously augment the more typical verbal or written instructions by pairing the words with the visual or sound input. Doing an example on the chalkboard while giving a verbal explanation, or having someone perform the act while others are seeing and hearing the directions are possibilities for this pairing.

Examples

- "Listen to what I'm thinking while I'm doing this problem. I can't subtract 7 from 3, so I need to regroup from the tens to the ones. I'll take a ten from _____" (while the work is being demonstrated on the chalkboard).
- "Listen carefully while I give directions and watch what I am doing."
- "Tell us what this graph is displaying."
- "Watch me and listen to what I am thinking as I make a *k*. I start at the top and make a straight line . . ."
- "Say to yourself what you're doing while you're imaging yourself doing it."

The importance of modeling cannot be overemphasized. Observational learning (see chapter 12) can result from "seeing someone else do it." Successful teachers have been using this technique for years, but only recently have we known the neurological reason why the dual input of seeing it combined with reading or hearing about it was such an effective educational strategy.

Teachers, purposefully and deliberately, need to pair visual-spatial information with verbal explanation. For example, "You see on this map, Oregon is above California and north is at the top of most maps. Oregon is closer to the top, or north of California." Combining input by pairing words with diagrams also can accelerate learning, "California had four times as much rainfall this year as it did last year, so if we left this bucket (sketched on chalkboard) out all last year and it filled up only to here (fill in a fourth with chalk), this year it would have filled to the top (fill in to top)." The possibilities are limited only by the teacher's ability to generate words and examples that are part of the learners' experience.

In many languages, the verbs *to show* and *to teach* are the same word. When teachers *show* what they mean by modeling and labeling a process, students have the opportunity for integrated hemispheric processing. "This is what I'm thinking about and deciding as I work this problem (make my outline). First I _____." Teachers also can show a product (paragraph, map, and so on) and label the critical elements. "See, here is the topic sentence and each sentence supports that main idea." Successful following of directions usually results when a student *hears the words* that tell what is to be done in a certain order and *sees* someone do it in that order. These techniques have always been used by effective teachers. Now we know why they are successful.

While the teacher can present information to both halves of the brain, it is the student who does the hemispheric processing. Therefore, it is critical that the teacher encourage the student to actively pursue *integrated* processing. The teacher may facilitate this processing; however, the student must construct the meaning or significance. The teacher can use prompts to encourage student thinking: "Try to visualize this," "How will you make sense of this?" "Will you remember better if you say it to yourself or make a diagram (outline)?"

Again, the caution needs to be sounded that possibilities are not realities, and the student may process perceptions by using only one hemisphere and disregard the potential assistance or possible interference from the other. (It should be noted that occasionally input to one hemisphere can interfere with the optimal functioning of the other. In that case, input would not be combined.)

2.   *Augmenting the Stimulus With Information for the Other Hemisphere.* When the student is not "getting it," follow information aimed at one hemisphere with information beamed to the other hemisphere.

Obviously, lack of facility with use of one hemisphere is only one of many possible reasons for learning difficulties. For any learner to be successful, the learning task must be at the right level of difficulty with all necessary subordinate learnings having already been achieved. The student should be motivated to exert learning effort. The learning should have been made meaningful and relevant to the student. Practice should be appropriate to the task and to the student. Changing hemispheric input systems, however, can sometimes remediate a learning problem. Here are some examples of providing alternate input.

Examples

- "Watch while I do one" (right hemisphere) or "You tell me what to do" (left hemisphere).
- "Look at this, now find another one like it" (right) or "I'll describe one, and you describe another one like it" (left).
- "Look carefully so you match yours to mine" (right) or "You say one similar to the one I say" (left).
- "Let's act one out, do one without talking" (right) or "Let's talk this one through" (left).
- "Make a picture of 6 x 7" (right) or "Describe this multiplication picture" (left).
- "Find it on the map" (right) or "Say what the map shows" (left).
- "We would graph it like this" (right) or "How would you interpret this graph?" (left).
- "If we put it on a time line, where would it be?" (right) or "If we translated the time line into words, we would say . . ." (left).
- "Show me what I should do" (right) or "Do what I say" (left).

3.   *Deliberate Beaming of Instruction to Only One Hemisphere.* Focusing on one hemisphere enables students to practice handling a situation in which they get only one kind of input, for it may occur throughout their lives—for example, hearing or reading without seeing, seeing without hearing or reading. Often, they are only "told," or they must read directions with no diagram, so that they must "see for themselves" what is meant. At other times, they may be asked to perform after "being shown," in which case they may need to "say to myself what I should do."

Examples

- "Read the directions and see if you can do it."
- "Look at the diagram and see if you can figure it out."
- "Look at this design and see if you can make one just like it."
- "Listen to my directions and see if you can make the figure I am describing."
- "Read the chapter and answer the questions."
- "Look at this sequence of three pictures and draw what the fourth might be."

4.   *Using Examples From the Student's Own Experience.* Whenever we use an experience from the learner's own life to illustrate a concept or a process, we are eliciting potential from students' *imaging* (not imagining), which can give a "right-brained assist" to input from a "left-brained" verbal generalization. For example, a teacher might explain, "*Persevere* means that you make yourself keep on doing something even though you are tempted to stop. As you worked on speeding up your number combinations last night, I suspect you got bored and wanted to stop and watch TV. If you made yourself keep on working, you persevered. If you kept on because your father or mother made you, you didn't persevere, because you weren't making yourself do it. Now think of an example of another time when you persevered, when you made yourself keep on doing something even though you wanted to stop." As a student uses the verbal definition of *persevere* to analyze his/her past experience and select an experience (left hemisphere), it is highly probable s/he will *see* or *hear* and *feel* that experience in his/her "mind's eye" (right hemisphere), thereby giving a *visual*, *auditory*, or *kinesthetic* assist to a verbal concept.

Computation in arithmetic is an outstanding example of learners' trying to remember a sequence of steps without a referent from their past experience. As a result, mathematics often has little meaning. A problem such as $4.25 divided by 85 usually stimulates temporal directions, "First I divide, then multiply, then subtract, then bring down."

Instead of the students' working solely from a temporal sequence of operations, the teacher should add the input of experience, "Suppose you had $4.25 and hamburgers cost 85 cents each. How many hamburgers could you buy for yourself and your friends?" This example surely carries more meaning and may even elicit an assumed "right-brained" assist of imaging ("Oh, I see what we're doing") from the student.

Asking students to generate examples from their own experiences is of great importance in giving learners the "assist" of using both hemispheres. Not only can this add imaging, which transfers learning from the past to give added meaning to the present experience, but it enables the teacher to check the accuracy and validity of the student's perception and understanding of the present learning. Here are some examples of having students make their own examples.

Examples

- "Make up a word problem that will go with 250 ÷ 25 = (or 4 + 8 =)."
- "What things would Goldilocks try in your house?"
- "What traits do you have that make you like Columbus?"
- "What have you done that is the same as _____?"

Not all important learning occurs in the classroom. Science involves integrating the brain processes of planning, measuring, preparing, implementing, monitoring, and inspecting results.

When students are encouraged to think back to their own experiences, it helps them "see" a concept or generalization, particularly when feelings are associated with that experience. In that case, most students automatically image (see in their "mind's eye") that experience, and integrated processing in both hemispheres is more likely. The added propulsion from *meaning* (the relation of the present concept to the individual's past experience or knowledge) should increase students' motivation to learn, the rate and degree of learning, as well as retention and the appropriate transfer of that learning to new situations, problem solving, and creative endeavors. (See chapter 15.) It is important that we recognize the many factors, besides use of knowledge of the function of brain hemispheres, that promote learning and not ignore other powerful accelerants to learning because we have discovered hemisphericity.

Conclusion

What, then, is our educational responsibility, we who are not neurologists, we who are not responsible for the reeducation of victims of accidents or of those who evidence brain pathology, but we who do have the important responsibility for making learning more probable, more predictably successful, more efficient and more effective for those millions of students, from preschool through postsecondary education, who are entrusted to our classroom guidance?

We must, of course, follow the paths of the researchers, translating, as soon as we are able, their findings into classroom practice. We must, with that translation, make available to every teacher (and student), in language s/he can understand, strategies that effectively and comfortably can be used in his/her classroom regardless of budget, organizational scheme, materials available, pupil-teacher ratio (granted all of those are important, but not determining variables). We must, in turn, present questions and concerns that will focus researchers on areas most productive in terms of learning gain for students. And finally, we must incorporate in our dissemination of important information, our acknowledgement that "we must practice what we preach" and develop left-brained and right-brained input of information, *modeling* by our own behavior the fact that neither hemisphere is superior to the other, neither is the chosen one, both are essential to integrated thinking. This world would be a better, more accepting, more stimulating, and more fulfilling place for all of us if we accepted the differences, recognized the similarities, and acknowledged the right to learn of all students. Therefore, as one beginning step, we must deliberately incorporate those strategies that reflect research in hemisphericity into our daily teaching and augment (not replace!) with right-brained input, the predominantly left-brained educational programs currently in our schools.

In summary,

1.   We should incorporate current knowledge about hemisphericity into our daily teaching so that students' have the advantage of *knowing* what is meant by reading or hearing *words* (augmented by oral clues from intonation and by written clues from punctuation) and *seeing* what is meant by *visuals* and *spatial* relationships.

2.   While we may control the input, we do not control the hemispheric processing in anyone's brain. The student may deliberately or subconsciously transfer processing to the other hemisphere.

3.   Facility in processing by either hemisphere is increased with practice. Therefore, we should provide many opportunities for "right-brained," "left-brained," and "integrated brained" learning so every student has a repertoire of processing responses, available for any learning situation, thereby becoming more facile in the deliberate use of those processing skills that best contribute to satisfying and successful achievement in a variety of situations.

4.   There are many factors besides hemisphericity operating in human learning. We need to become aware of as many as possible and use them deliberately and purposefully in teaching.

5.   Knowledge of hemisphericity provides one more small piece in the puzzle of human learning. As we add that piece to our complex array of decisions and practice in teaching, we may promote increasingly effective results.

Bibliography

Baron, J. B., & Sternberg, R. J. (Eds.). (1987). *Teaching thinking skills: Theory and practice.* New York: W. H. Freeman.

Costa, A. (Ed.). (1985). *Developing minds.* Alexandria, VA: Association for Supervision and Curriculum Development.

Hawk, D. P. (1986). Using graphic organizers to increase achievement in middle school life science. *Science Education, 70*(1), 81–87.

Hunter, M. (1976). Right-brained kids in left-brained schools. *Today's Education,* (Nov./Dec.).

Keehe, J. W. (1987). *Learning style theory and practice.* Reston, VA: National Association of Elementary School Principals.

Manning, N. (1986). *Brain Theory and Learning, 60,* 127–130.

McCarthy, B. (1987). The Format System. *Teaching to learning styles.* Barrington, IL: Excel.

11

The Chalkboard: An Assist to Both Hemispheres

"The way you're using that chalkboard is an affront to students' right hemispheres" was the criticism leveled at a teacher.

"Well," was the teacher's indignant defense, "nobody ever taught me how to use a chalkboard."

"Nobody ever taught *anybody* how to use a chalkboard" was the supervisor's retort.

"Well, why haven't they?" queried the teacher. "When every teacher in the world uses a chalkboard, why haven't you teacher educators taught us how to do it?"

Why indeed? Because nobody ever thought to teach the skill and theory behind one of education's most common tools and practices.

131

It is analytic, theory-based thought about what teachers do to increase the probability of learning that has become the hallmark of education as a profession. A professional emerges when theory-based knowledge is artistically implemented by a person who also makes the modifications to theory that are indicated by the needs of the client (student), as well as by the content and situation.

Let's examine the theory-based knowledge we now possess that would influence our use of the ubiquitous chalkboard. Research on the functioning of the brain has revealed that most people process information *sequentially and analytically* in their left hemispheres. In contrast, they process *visual-spatial* relationships *simultaneously* in their right hemispheres. The chalkboard affords us the opportunity to present oral or written language (processed in the left hemisphere) augmented by visual spatial relationships (processed in the right hemisphere), thereby encouraging integrated hemispheric processing. It is no accident that we use the expression "I see what you mean." The chalkboard helps a student visually see relationships among verbal concepts or information.

To use a chalkboard effectively, you need to be guided by four basic principles. Some of them you know intuitively, but by bringing

The way a chalkboard is used has the power to turn students on—or off!

them to a conscious level, you can deliberately and successfully build each principle into your daily teaching. How to do this is covered in the rest of the chapter.

1. Say Before Writing

The first principle of chalkboard use is based on three assumptions:

- We can say something faster than we can write it. Consequently, when we say it, most students can immediately begin processing the information in their left hemispheres and do not have to wait until meaning begins to emerge from the words being written.
- Students do not have to predict or "guess" the next words or the meaning (possibly erroneously) as they try to complete the not-yet finished message while it is being written.
- The silence during the time necessary to write on the chalkboard provides the seconds neurologically necessary from initial perception of the words or message to processing of that information in working memory. When one message or idea is followed immediately by another, it is possible for the second idea to eradicate the first. A few seconds of silence enables students to process and store a message in the memory "bank" for later retrieval.

Consequently, most of the time we should say what we are going to write on the chalkboard before writing it. Obviously, if for some reason we wish the student to see a message emerge, or to attempt to guess the complete message, or to be responsible for reading it, we will write without first stating what we are going to write.

2. Use Key Words and Simple Diagrams

It is important that students focus on the key concepts or central ideas of what is being presented. While we may elaborate on these concepts or ideas in speech, the key ideas should stand out on the chalkboard and not be lost in the clutter of words. Consequently, we write as few words as possible to preserve the meaning. When we make a diagram, it should be simple so relationships are easily perceived. By using key words and simple diagrams, we make it possible for the student's right hemisphere to process what is seen, while the left hemisphere processes the elaboration provided by our words. The integration of those two functions should contribute to more effective learning and retention.

Examples

- We *say*, "On your chalkboard, use key words and simple diagrams."

  We *write* only "Key words—simple diagrams."

- We *say*, "Washington was our first elected president."

  We *write*, "Washington—1st president."

- We *say*, "Pamela had a pizza cut in fourths. She gave one fourth to Tom."

  We *write*,

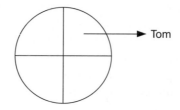

- We *say*, "Alligators have rounded noses or snouts. Crocodiles have thin pointed snouts."

  We *write*,

3. Position = Relationship

The chalkboard provides the opportunity to indicate relationships between concepts and ideas through their position in two-dimensional space, a relationship that can be processed in the student's right hemisphere. An outline is an excellent example of position in space indicating relationships. Look at the following outline:

    I.   Techniques in Teaching
         A. Use of chalkboard
         B. Use of overhead
         C. Use of complex visuals

The position of A, B, and C indicates they are parallel ideas that are subsets of, but not as inclusive or important as, roman numeral I. The position in space of the items in an outline provides an important visual cue to help clarify the relationship of ideas.

If, on our chalkboard, we write—

Washington
Adams
Jefferson

we imply that Washington comes first in some order (election, to be studied, discussed, and so on).

If we write—

Washington   Adams   Jefferson

we imply there is a parallel or oppositional relationship, not (unless we number them) a first, second, third relationship. Arrows, lines, simple diagrams also indicate (to the right hemisphere) the relationship of the items on the chalkboard.

When we are aware of the power of position in space to suggest relationships, we avoid placing items on the chalkboard in a haphazard fashion or wherever there happens to be space. We place each item deliberately so that its position indicates its relationship to other material on the chalkboard (causal, oppositional, numerical, comparative, categorical, and so on).

Saying *and* showing are important for integrated brain processing.

4. Erase Before Introducing a New Concept

In the same way that a clear head encourages clear thinking, a clean chalkboard encourages effective learning. So the final principle in chalkboard use is to erase everything that is not necessary before you proceed to the next idea. Erasing "holes" in what is already on the chalkboard so that something else can be added, erasing that leaves bits and pieces of previous ideas, writing between other ideas, utilizing every inch of space—all constitute "right hemispheric atrocities" because what you are presenting gets lost in the visual competition for attention. You would not try to talk to students when there is a lot of interfering noise. Don't try to write on your chalkboard when there is a lot of interfering clutter.

Sometimes, teachers do not erase because they do not want to waste the time necessary to clean a board. They are wise to realize that each precious minute should be spent focused on learning. However, a simple solution to that dilemma is to give the students something to think about or to do while you are erasing.

A clean chalkboard makes for clear learning.

Examples
"While I am erasing this—
- Be ready to state the four principles of chalkboard use."
- Make up a word problem that would require you to multiply."
- Be ready to state in one sentence what you consider to be an important facet of Washington's personality."
- Say to yourself, your own definition of _____."

Using this technique will (1) stimulate the student to review what has been learned, (2) hold him/her accountable for evidence of that learning, and (3) give you time to clean the board so the next idea is just as clear visually as it is in your verbal presentation.

Conclusion

There are times, of course, when the simplicity of the chalkboard is not as effective as the motivational impact or the time saved by using prepared visuals. Neither chalkboard nor prepared visuals are good in and of themselves; it's how they are used and for what purpose that determine their effectiveness. It is the prerogative of the teacher to decide whether the simplicity of basic information presented verbally and accompanied by clear visuals on a chalkboard will better promote learning, or whether the vividness, accuracy, and reality provided by realia, pictures, and motion pictures will be more enabling.

Clearly, the decision is yours. Remember, however, when you use that ubiquitous chalkboard, your use should reflect awareness that in most (not all) cases you do these:

1. Say before writing.
2. Use key words and simple diagrams.
3. Demonstrate position = relationship.
4. Erase before introducing a new concept.

These same principles apply to the use of an overhead projector.

In all cases, the goal is to use the classroom tools effectively so as a result, left-brained, right-brained, integrated learning results.

12

Observational Learning

"Learning by doing" became the credo of schools during the first half of the twentieth century. Because overt participation by the student had previously been neglected and it was believed that performance behaviors would not be learned unless the student "did" them, an erroneous assumption was made that "doing" was always the best way to learn. Everyday observation should have convinced us that this was not true. Many people have "done" things for years and still do not do them very well; witness driving, cooking, teaching, playing a musical instrument, painting, sports, and so on. Obviously, just doing something does not predictably yield excellence in performance. If the doer's performance is to improve, doing must be subject to sophisticated scrutiny by the doer, the assistance from a "knowledgeable other," or the presence of a model who is emulated.

Definition of Observational Learning

"Doing" has come under scrutiny recently from another quarter where psychologists are finding that watching another person "do" can have a profound effect on the future performance of the observer. The opportunity for *observational learning* is a powerful factor in efficient progression toward improved performance. Observational learning can be defined as behavior that is learned or modified as the result of observing the behavior of others.

Research in the operation of the hemispheres of the brain also indicates that the acquisition of learning by visual-spatial and auditory input—seeing a model do something while the model comments on what s/he is doing—is preferred and more readily assimilated by some learners than merely listening to an explanation or reading about it. Observational learning can be an enabling precursor to effectively doing it oneself.

An interesting (and sometimes lethal) factor in observational learning is that it often occurs when the learner has no intention of learning or has minimal motivation to learn. Observational learning also seems to occur just as effectively in large groups as it does in the smaller, more intimate groups, which we tend to think should be better learning situations. With educators' current concern with humanistic and world-view education, it is important to stress that many values, attitudes, and beliefs are acquired through observational learning.

We see the phenomenon of observational learning occurring everywhere. Television is one of our most powerful sources of teaching by modeling. Students emulate the behavior of TV personalities (hair, clothes, expressions, products used, and so on). Whenever students take the role of teachers or parents, we see them exhibit behavior that is the same as the person they have observed in that role. That behavior has not been taught or practiced; it has been acquired through observational learning, even though the observer seemingly had no conscious intention to learn the modeled behavior. Merely observing a model exhibit a response can increase the likelihood that the observer will exhibit the same response.

Seeing someone else give a response also seems to lower the threshold of resistance of the observer to make a similar response, enabling the response to come forth more readily. To cite an example, we all have

Observation is a powerful way of acquiring knowledge and behavior.

observed how difficult it is to get someone in an audience to ask the first question of the speaker, and how subsequent questions follow more readily once the "ice has been broken." This is because the questioning behavior has been modeled. Lynching mobs and gossiping groups are examples of negative models bringing forth responses that usually are suppressed but that emerge as a result of seeing someone else perform those behaviors. Modeling also can provide critical information by showing how another person handles a situation that we might encounter in the future or have encountered in the past. Therefore, modeling is an important source in the process of information giving.

Conditions Affecting Observational Learning

There is no question that a great deal of everyone's learning is acquired from observation. Learning to talk is an obvious example. Since modeling has such a profound influence on the probability of either positive or negative learning by the learner, it behooves educators to know the conditions under which observational learning is most likely to occur and to take advantage of those conditions so that they yield efficient and productive results for the observer.

Here are descriptions of the conditions that seem to affect observational learning.

1. The attributes of the model will affect the probability that his/her behavior will be reproduced. There must be some kind of interactive relationship, real or fancied, between the observer and the model for the latter's behavior to "teach" the observer. The observer must identify with the model (a peer-group member, or someone who has actually experienced his/her problems such as fellow weight watchers/dieters), or the model must possess some characteristic (status or possessions) that the observer admires or respects (a social or political leader, star athlete, television figure). The attributes of a model who has "made it" become the magic talisman for the observer who also wants to "make it." An example of the power of modeling by significant others occurred in a girl's school in Virginia when, for a study, three high-status, admired seniors dressed differently and unbecomingly. In only three weeks, 78% of the student body were dressing in the same unbecoming way.

The power of modeling is derived from the presence of some emotional tie—the interactive relationship of social or emotional identification with the model. This tie causes the observer to think, feel, and act as s/he imagines the model does. This identification is particularly important in learning to conform to social norms and in learning strong emotions such

Imitation is the beginning of developing more complex observational skills.

The intent to acquire the model's behavior accelerates observational learning.

as fear. Often modeling is defined as the process of "social influence." It is important to realize that the educational impetus from wanting to "be like friends or like the teacher" can counteract the influence of some out-of-school environments where there are no productive models.

It is also critical to realize that moral development can be an important outcome of modeling. Social learning theorists have demonstrated that observation of models such as teachers, parents, and peers can influence a child's adoption of moral standards. Students' moral behavior also can be influenced by their perception of the consequences that others have incurred for moral and immoral acts. This topic is discussed in more detail in point 3, below.

When a student makes a moral judgment and a "significant other" models the opposite behavior, there can be a profound effect on that student's next judgment of appropriate behavior. Praising his/her moral judgment will be relatively ineffective if s/he observes the opposite behavior being modeled. For example, in a room with toys s/he is not supposed to touch, if a child sees a model touch and "get away with it," s/he is likely to succumb.

The observer's former training in personal standards is weakened if a significant model doesn't follow these standards. The observational learner breaks rules in proportion to the number of others s/he sees breaking them. S/he follows rules in proportion to the number of others s/he sees following them. This phenomenon is documented by the presence of litter on the school grounds or in the lavatories. When paper is thrown on the grounds or floor, it continues to accrue. If there is no paper scattered around, students tend to discard it appropriately into receptacles. This is why graffiti needs to be removed as quickly as possible.

    2.   *When the behavior observed is possible for the observer to emulate, the probability of observational learning is increased.* At times, it may be better that the model display gradual acquisition of a skill rather than perfect performance at the outset. This way the observer does not become discouraged by the gap between the behavior that currently is possible for him/her and the polished performance of the model. Teachers should be aware that sometimes modeled behavior should include both the terminal "excellent" response and also the responses that occur earlier in the chain of behavioral acquisition. Modeling the next thing in the series to be learned is a productive way to encourage observational learning. The teacher should make a considered decision as to whether to model the "perfect" performance for motivational reasons, the next step in improved performance, or both types of performance. No one decision is always correct.

    It is reassuring to those of us who have to model or to provide models to note that the model does not have to be a paragon. However, the model must be credible to the observer, as well as be one with whom the learner can identify. If the model is perceived as having such a high standard that it seems impossible for the observer to attain that standard, s/he may reject the model.

    3.   *The possibility of the learner's imitated response may be strengthened or weakened depending on what happens to the model as a result of the modeled behavior.* If the person performing the behavior to be achieved is rewarded, the observer is encouraged to imitate that behavior, providing it is possible for him/her. If the behavior is seen as too difficult, however, rewarding the model may discourage the observer. If the person performing the behavior is punished, imitation tends to be discouraged. Behavior that is not rewarded or punished is less effective in influencing the observer. Therefore, a critical component of observational learning is the vicarious effect of the consequences and outcomes that happen to the model. This is an important generalization for teachers to keep in mind when they expect modeled behavior to be imitated or avoided.

    4.   *The observer's response is also influenced by what happens to him/her as a result of producing the imitated behavior.* It becomes important, therefore, that teachers reinforce *specific,* desirable imitated behavior on the part of observers as soon as it occurs. This reinforcement not only gives the observational learner the necessary feedback for the imi-

Some things are better taught by demonstration than by diagrams or words.

tative behavior but makes the reoccurrence of that behavior more probable when the model no longer is present.

 5. *The observer's imitative response is strengthened by behavioral rehearsal.* Often a learner needs to be given a chance to role-play a response after observation so that the response becomes a familiar part of his/her repertoire. Simulation is a type of behavioral rehearsal that makes for faster and more predictable learning. Research indicates that one (not the only) effective way to learn a new behavior is to watch someone else perform that behavior and then try to imitate it. Even behaviors that are difficult to change, such as fear, respond to a model who demonstrates mastery and lack of fear in a situation. Models can have a positive effect on long-standing behavior, such as fear of snakes (watching someone handle them with no problem) and test anxiety (watching someone demonstrate an efficient and worklike approach to taking a test).

An important classroom example of productive behavior that has resulted from opportunities for observational learning is the asking of clarifying questions during instruction. Learning to identify one's confusion and do something about it (an important objective for all learners) responds positively to demonstration. Suppose someone in class asks a successful clarifying question (producing a model), followed by the teacher's reinforcing response to the question. This can lead an observer to produce a similar behavior. The teacher should reinforce the observer's new behavior: "Sara, that was an important question that clarified it for the rest of us."

To deal with the problem of changing an already established behavior, modeling can be helpful when there is an articulated and clear picture of what the student is doing that is maladaptive, a model of the substitute behavior that would produce more desirable consequences, a rehearsal of the new behavior with reinforcement in a simulated situation, and finally the production of that behavior, if at all possible, in a "real" situation with reinforcement. For example, watching a friend handle his/her anger with words instead of fists, practicing in a simulated situation some phrases that could be used when aggression is evoked, then being reinforced for the more productive response in a "real" situation is an excellent prescription for developing alternatives to fighting.

Planning for Observational Learning

There is no question of the power of "seeing someone else do." However, if observational learning is to occur by design rather than happenstance, the teacher should do the following:

1. Define as explicitly as possible the type of behavior to be modeled.
2. Determine and articulate for the learner the conditions under which a student would make the response and those conditions under which the response would not be appropriate. Identifying the critical attribute when one *should* and *should not* avoids

inappropriate blind imitation. (Unfortunately, this critical discrimination often is not developed in teacher education.)

3. Design a learning opportunity that will enable the learner to
   practice discriminating between the two sets of conditions.
4. Present modeling that is as clear and unambiguous as possible, with a model with whom the learner can identify.
5. Determine and design the observer's behavioral rehearsals:
   what kind, how many?
6. Implement the observational learning opportunity. Reinforce
   both the model and the imitator, making sure that correct cues
   are being perceived and articulated.
7. Determine appropriate instructional strategies that utilize
   research-based principles of learning that will improve or
   strengthen all of this teaching.

While it is important that students "figure things out for themselves," it is equally important that their discriminators (knowing when
something is appropriate and when it is not) be systematically developed and that they be shown examples of productive behavior. Whenever
a person knows what needs to be done but doesn't know how to do it, seeing the behavior modeled while the observer is focused on and attending
to appropriate and relevant elements of that modeling will assist the
observer in acquiring the behavior.

As the power of observational learning continues to be documented,
it is important to note that much of the performance behavior in the
process of successful teaching can be initially acquired by teachers
through observation of videotaped and live models. Then that knowledge can be refined and reinforced by behavioral rehearsal and finally
polished by practice in the reality of the classroom—practice that is
monitored, analyzed, and coached for further improvement by sophisticated educational observers.

For the continuously needed, professional renewal of the educator in the field, it is also important that all educators not only "hear or
read about it." but see new techniques modeled by videotape or "live
teaching" in order to more readily acquire sophisticated and effective
professional behaviors so these behaviors become a part of their professional repertoires. Practice, which continues to be monitored, coached,
reinforced, and refined, will ensure the stability and automaticity of
those behaviors in the observers' future educational practice.

In summary, research in observational learning mandates that an
educator's choice is either to understand and guide observational learning or to permit it to take place haphazardly, with the possibility that
unproductive as well as productive behaviors are observed and learned.

Bibliography

Baldwin, A. L. (1973). Social learning. In F. Kerlinger (Ed.), *Review of Research in Education* (Vol. 4, pp. 34–57). Itasca, Il: Peacock.

Bandura, A. (1977). *Social learning theory.* Englewood Cliffs, N J: Prentice-Hall.

Brophy, J. (1988). Research linking teacher behavior to student achievement: Potential implications for instruction of Chapter I students. *Educational Psychology, 23*(3), 235–286.

Caroll, W., & Bandura, A. (1982). The role of visual monitoring in observation learning in action patterns: Making the unobservable observable. *Journal of Motor Behavior, 14,* 153–167.

Doyle, W. (1986). Classroom organization and management. In M. C. Wittrock (Ed.), *Handbook of research on teaching* (3rd ed., pp. 392–431). New York: Macmillan.

Jeffery, R. S. (1976). The influence of symbolic and motor rehearsal in observational learning. *Journal of Research in Personality, 10,* 117–126.

Schunk, D. H. (1981). Modeling and attributional effects on children's achievement: A self-efficacy analysis. *Journal of Educational Psychology, 73,* 93–105.

Section

4

Decisions About Teaching Behaviors

Of all school factors that promote students' successful learning, the professional skills of teachers are the most powerful. Teaching skills are more important than books, equipment, and materials, and we certainly need all these excellent resources. Teaching skills are more important than budget, and heaven knows education

151

is underbudgeted. Teaching skills are more important than facilities, and we need attractive, safe facilities. Teaching skills are even more important than pupil-teacher ratio, and we're all for a low pupil-teacher ratio. But more powerful than any of these highly desirable factors are the professional skills of the teacher to encourage and facilitate students' academic, social, emotional, and physical achievement and to produce students who will be successful lifelong learners with a continuing zest for learning.

No longer is it possible for a teacher to acquire only a few generic skills. A full repertoire of skills in making effective decisions in content, learning behaviors, and teaching behaviors must be possessed by the teacher, who then implements those decisions with artistry and creativity.

These professional skills are discussed in more depth in many books and videotapes (see the bibliography at the end of chapter 1). In this section, only a few skills that all relate to teaching will be described.

Chapter 13 indicates techniques whereby time can be used more effectively to maximize students' learning. Time is our "coin" in teaching, and many teachers feel bankrupt. Time can be spent wisely, or it can be frittered away on busywork or inconsequential tasks.

Chapter 14 emphasizes the power of examples to accelerate learning by building connections between new learning and the students' long-term memories. Because of this power, teachers need to use the critical attributes of effective examples (outlined in the chapter) to analyze their own examples.

Chapter 15 addresses the meaningfulness of what is being learned and highlights our national deficit in the development of students who comprehend and enjoy math. Mathematical understanding (numeracy), kindergarten through high school, can be attained by almost all students with average intelligence. Yet, math is feared and avoided by most. The most pervasive reason is that students "do it" but don't have the foggiest notion of why they are doing what they are doing, and what it means in terms of the quantitative relationships that must be dealt with on an everyday basis. The principles involved in generating meaning can be, and should be, incorporated into any content, including math content.

Chapter 16 focuses on effective ways to assist students with the "nuts and bolts" of vocabulary development and gaining automaticity with basic math facts. An assignment to "look it up in the dictionary and memorize the definition" ought to be actionable in court! Equally inefficient is an admonition to "work on all your basic facts."

The next four chapters—chapters 17, 18, 19, 20—are extrapolations from research, and they discuss solutions to prevailing problems in teaching: how to help students who are having difficulty learning, teachers' ubiquitous use of "I," teachers' habit of repeating students' answers, and how to teach the critical social skill of "disagreeing agreeably."

Chapter 21 provides techniques that release teachers from the bonds of interminable paper correcting yet increase their ability to monitor "how students are doing." It presents techniques for assessing students' achievement *while* teaching.

Chapter 22 addresses the controversial topic of the value of homework and suggests assignments that are of interest to students as well as being growth-evoking for them rather than being ineffective drudgery.

Chapter 23 clarifies the relationship between teaching and testing. Its goal is to enable teachers to realize maximum benefits from assessing students' achievements of desirable outcomes, as well as suggesting ways assessment might be accomplished efficiently and effectively.

This book concludes with a chapter on the importance of the professionals in education and identifies their critical contributions to the future of our global society and to the world we currently inhabit.

chapter

13

Efficient Use of Time for Effective Learning[1]

Time is the coin of teaching. That is what we have to spend to obtain learning. We can spend that time wisely on quality learning, or we can fritter it away, when students waste time waiting or doing busywork. It may be better for students to do busywork (memorize trivia, copy the questions before they write the answers, do 20 of the same kind of problem) than to do nothing, but busywork can result in students' concluding that school is boring, tedious, and mindless. School

[1]This chapter was written in collaboration with Rob Hunter, principal of a Chapter I school in Simi, CA.

155

Waiting time can become learning time by having students think about or do something during transitions.

should be a place where the excitement of learning something important prevails.

School districts all over the nation are extending the school day and year to gain more instructional time. An analysis of the way our present allotment of time is expended reveals that a great deal of the time already available is being wasted. As a result, in a school year of the same number of days, students who have an efficient and effective teacher may receive the equivalent of many more days of instruction than do those unfortunate students where many minutes in each school day become wasted time.

"Time leaks" can occur during three different phases of the teaching/learning process:

1. Transition time
2. Instructional time
3. Postinstruction, independent practice time

During each of these three phases, potential time leaks can be plugged when students are *taught* to maximize use of that time for generating meaning, thinking, and learning. Notice that the verb is "taught," not "told" or "admonished."

Transition Time

When students enter the classroom, there is an interval that varies from one to several minutes before instruction can begin. The more skilled the teacher, the shorter is this interval. Students, however, do come from different parts of the grounds and buildings, and so they arrive in "spread-out time." Also, there can be unexpected, initial interruptions: parents, notes, visitors, or discipline problems. Attendance procedures, collection of money or papers, and distribution of materials also may need the teacher's attention. All of this administrivia may delay instruction at the beginning of class.

The most important "stopper" for this time leak is to determine whether such initial administrative tasks are really necessary at the beginning of the period, or whether they could be handled after students are productively engaged. Most of these initial delays are avoidable. When students know that something worthwhile and important will happen as soon as they enter the class, most will hurry to get there to participate. Even with the best planning, however, all students cannot magically appear in class at the same instant, and certain delays (very few!) are unavoidable. One effective stopper of this time leak is to *teach* students to start working on learning tasks—which can be previously planned—as soon as they enter the room. Some examples include these: follow previous directions to review yesterday's notes, check homework from an answer key on the board, do prereading of materials for today's assignment, work on number facts or spelling words previously missed, or read a library book available in the student's desk. Any similar activities can serve the important purpose of utilizing transition time for learning.

Another productive way to use transition time is to have directions on the chalkboard, or some place equally visible, to start students' thinking or working as soon as they enter the room. Here are some examples of chalkboard activities:

- Be ready to describe the properties of plants that we discussed yesterday.
- Think of a word problem from your life that would match this equation: $x + 2x + 5x =$
- Be ready to define (in your own words) these terms: _____
- Count and list how many things you can see in this room that begin with a consonant blend. Be ready to name them.
- Write a five-sentence summary paragraph about _____.
- Take this five-minute test: _____.

Even young students can follow directions in cartoon form directing them to "read a book," "go to the listening center," "come to the rug," once the students are *taught* to do so. The possibilities are limited only by what students have learned to do and by the skill of the teacher to elicit students' motivated utilization of learning time.

Having visible directions that list materials needed, and how to secure them, also stops time leaks that occur in typical classroom distribution procedures. Examples: "Take a book from the table—you'll need paper and pencil." "Read pages 17 to 21 and write a 'hard question' about what you've read."

Pocket charts or alphabetical name files stationed around the room to avoid traffic jams (A–G in front, H–M on the side, and so on) enable students of all ages to take their own attendance and to deposit their envelopes of lunch money or returned notes, so that administrative time leaks are diminished and the teacher is free to do more important things.

The transitional, learning activities are called "sponges" because they productively "sop up" waiting time and use it for needed practice: time that would otherwise be wasted in waiting until instruction can begin. Having students productively engaged rather than socializing or getting into trouble usually gives a teacher discipline-free minutes to gather materials, handle a problem if needed, answer notes, or do anything else that should not be delayed. In addition, sponge activities give students practice in directing themselves rather than always being lead into what to do.

Instructional Time

Two inexcusable time leaks that can occur during instruction are—

1. The learning task is too easy, students already can do it or could do it without instruction, or the task is too difficult because prior, necessary learnings have not been accomplished. In either case, students and teachers are wasting time.
2. Ineffective or inefficient methods are being used to accomplish the learning. Examples of ineffective methods are poor directions, related but nonrelevant material included in the lesson, unfocused students, not enough or too many examples.

Time leaks can result from ineffective or insufficient preservice or inservice education for teachers, plus lack of coaching and supervision. Teachers can learn the skills needed to quickly diagnose students for appropriate levels of task difficulty, to analyze the learning task to determine what to include or exclude from this lesson, to plan and deliver directions that are easily followed, to elicit students' attention and motivation to learn throughout instruction, and to utilize principles of learning in order to plan and deliver effective instruction that maximizes student gain from time allotted. Cause-effect relationships in teaching and learning have been identified (see the bibliography at the end of chapter 1), and teachers can become proficient in these essential skills.

Let's examine some additional, less obvious instructional time leaks and some professional "stoppers" for these leaks.

Leak: Including material in a lesson that is related and could be important in another lesson, but is not necessary to achieve today's learning

Example: Spending time on identification of main idea when today's objective is locating information

Stopper: Perform a task analysis to determine the skills necessary for achievement of the learning and then sequence those skills in instruction. Leave the tempting, additional "desirable and important issues" for a subsequent lesson. (See chapter 5.)

Example: "Skim through until you find the three magic items the boy possessed."

Leak: Going on "by-the-way bird walks," or digressions, which can become distracting to the students

Example: When the objective is location skills in reading, encouraging students to deflect attention by telling their own experiences in similar situations or permitting the lesson to get derailed by students' unrelated comments. For example, saying, "Tell about something you sold." (This does not mean the teachers should not solicit students' experiences when doing so is appropriate.)

Stopper: Make the information, questions, and student activities relate directly to the instructional objective. Teaching is not rigid; you can always change objectives or add additional material when the situation indicates you should. Add participation, humor, and lilt that *contribute* to students' achievement rather than deflect their attention to unrelated issues.

Example: "Find the sentence that describes how the boy felt when he sold the pony. What do you think caused him to feel this way?"

Leak: Presenting material in such a way that students see no relevance to themselves. Consequently, they aren't motivated to put forth learning effort.

Example: "Democracy means rule by the majority."

Stopper: Create interest in concepts and skills by relating them to what those students already know and have experienced so motivation increases and learning outcomes are seen as interesting and important.

Example: "Which decisions in your family (class, club, group of friends) are or are not made democratically? Do you agree they should be?"

Leak: Passing out materials one at a time to each student

Example: "Mary, will you give everyone a paper?"

Stopper: Develop "distribution processes" that use minimal time, such as presented in the following examples.

Examples:

•   Having students pick up materials when they enter the class

When students know what they are doing and why they are doing it, their effective use of time is assured.

- The teacher reading the first question on the test before distributing test papers so students can be thinking of the answer and are ready to start writing the minute they get their papers
- The teacher writing the page number on the board and telling students what they should be considering or looking for in the chapter before books are distributed from several points in the group

Leak: Naming the student who will answer, before asking a question

Example: "John, what is the answer to question 5?" The other students, not needing to think, simply wait, with their minds "out of gear."

Stopper: Direct the question to the entire group so that all students feel accountable. Give them thinking time and get a response from each student, using techniques such as having everyone signal the answer or say it to a neighbor while you circulate to sample responses. In this way, every student answers almost every question and you find out who knows and who needs further explanation.

Example: "Look at the first sentence and be ready to signal a comma with your finger if it needs a comma or a zero for no comma, and state your reason."

Leak: Interruptions from the public address system with unnecessary announcements or with messages that could have waited until the end of the period

Examples: "Today's cafeteria menu is _____." "Will Paula come to the office for her sweater?" "The debate club will meet at the bus in front of school at three o'clock."

Stopper: Messages over the public address system should interrupt a class *only* in an emergency. Almost all other messages can be delivered by weekly or daily bulletins or individual notes. When announcements are unavoidable, schedule them at the end of a period so that students can be thinking about them at a time when they are not focused on classwork. Information for students can be posted in strategic places throughout the school. If a color code is used for each activity (menu—white, glee club—green, debate team—blue), students quickly learn to take responsibility and look for information that concerns them.

For classroom interruptions that are unavoidable (an important note from the office, an unanticipated visitor), give the students something to do or think about before you attend to the interruption. "Be ready to state three reasons why you think they chose Washington for president" or "Write a summary statement of our discussion so far." Then take care of the interruption while students are thinking and preparing their answers.

For emergency interruptions (fire drills, overturned fish tank), when things return to normal, ask students to think back and be ready to state what they were learning or doing just before the interruption. This assignment has high probability for teaching students the essential skill of taking their attention off the interruption and focusing it back on the lesson. If *you* state what they were doing, many will remain fixated on the interruption.

Leak: Having students work on tasks so difficult that no amount of effort will result in success or so easy that little or no effort is required

Examples:

- "Learn all your times tables."
- "Read the entire book and be ready to discuss it."

Stopper: Diagnose where students' learning leaves off and new learning needs to begin. Design instructional objectives at the correct level of difficulty so that students, with reasonable effort, can be successful. Break complex tasks into reasonable assignments.

Examples:

- "You know all but your nines; now you're ready to learn them."
- "Read the first chapter and be ready to describe the setting of the story."

Leak: Disciplining a student while the others "enjoy the show"

Example: "Bill, how many times must I tell you _____."

Stopper: Discipline privately. If the infraction is obvious to the class, handle it with a brief statement to the student, "We won't take class time for that now. We'll discuss it at the end of the period." When delay in handling the problem is not appropriate, give the other students something to do (solve a problem, write a brief paragraph, work with their neighbors to develop an example from their own lives) while you *privately* handle the problem.

Example: "Summarize with your neighbor the most important aspects of the _____ and be ready to state them." This gives you time to privately handle the culprit.

During instruction, any ineffective teacher/student behavior or interruption consumes time and energy and results in less learning. Deliberate reduction of these time leaks plus effective teaching can eliminate most of the lost time, maximize students' engagement and thinking, and result in increased interest and achievement by all students.

Postinstruction: Independent Practice Time

Frequently, after instruction, students practice what they have just learned. Time leaks can occur during independent practice. Here are some possible leaks and related stoppers.

Leak: Having students spend time on practice and activities that produce little learning gain

Examples: Copying the question before answering it, writing a spelling word 25 times, doing 20 of the same kind of problem, remaining so long on a task that boredom or inattention results

Stopper: Determine which activities contribute to the learning to be accomplished and how much repetition is necessary (usually not more than three to five repetitions at a time), thereby maximizing achievement gain for the time and energy expended. Doing five examples each day for five days will produce greater learning and retention than will 25 examples in one assignment.

Examples: Writing only the answer to the question. Practicing only two (for younger learners) to five spelling words at one time. Short, intense practice periods (5 to 10 of the same kind of problems) keep interest and intent to learn at a high level. More than 10 causes most students to put their brain in "neutral" and to stop attending to what they're doing.

Leak: Students not knowing when their answers are incorrect so they continue to make the same errors and the errors become "set"

Stopper: Teach students to use answer keys and teachers' answer books or to check with a "student teacher" so they can get immediate feedback and build in needed correction, thereby eliminating, for both student and teacher, a great deal of need-less work.

Example: "When you finish your first two, check with the key so that you know you're doing them correctly."

Leak: Students not knowing what to do after they finish a task

Stopper: Include in your directions the choices, tasks, and so on, that students have available to them when they finish their assignments. There should be routine procedures that students follow when they finish early so they become responsibly self-directing.

Examples:

- "When you finish, you'll find your options listed on the board."
- "Work on something you need to practice."

Leak: Students getting "stuck" during an assignment and needing assistance. The teacher is busy with another group and students have not been taught the sources for help aside from the teacher. Consequently they sit and wait, wasting their learning time.

Stopper: Teach self-help techniques such as rereading "slowly and softly out loud to yourself" to better understand, as well as *having students practice* the use of alternative sources of assistance such as other students, reference books, and so on.

Example: "Pretend you're stuck. What are some things you might do to help yourself or secure help? Let's practice them."

Leak: Students using the prime review time at the end of the period for cleanup with no thinking task

Example: "As soon as you clean up, take your seat."

Stopper: Ask students to do a quick mental review of what was learned so that after they have cleaned up, they can summarize what they have learned or be ready to state which part they thought was most important or enjoyable. Or, build a bridge to the next lesson by saying, "For tomorrow, be thinking of _____."

Example: "While you're cleaning up, get ready to state the steps in _____."

Leak: Students spending excessive (and frequently *unnecessary*) time lining up

Stopper: Dismiss students a few at a time as they answer review questions (after having *taught* them to get to and from their

Students can generate examples from their own experience, summarizing, reading for information, or working with a neighbor while their teacher deals with an interruption.

destination by themselves in an orderly fashion). If they must line up, have them answering questions, generating ideas, practicing something as the lines are forming rather than having students merely "packing up" and getting ready to leave.

Example: "Be thinking of the answers to these questions as you're excused to line up. I may call on someone in the line or someone still at his or her seat."

Conclusion

Examination of teachers' use of time indicates that many teaching hours are being wasted when they could be used effectively to promote students' learning. If time leaks during transitions, during instruction, and after instruction are eliminated, not only will discipline problems lessen, but substantial gains in academic learning time can be realized without adding a dollar to the budget, a minute to the school day, or a day to the school year. Deliberately stopping time leaks will result in realizing the major dividends of efficient and effective learning. The only cost is professional know-how.

Bibliography

Brophy, J., & Good, T. L. (1986). Teacher behavior and student achievement. In M. C. Wittrock (Ed.), *Handbook of research on teaching* (3rd ed.) New York: Macmillan.

Good, T. L., & Brophy, J. (1987). *Looking in classrooms* (4th ed., pp. 42–80). New York: Harper & Row.

Guskey, T. R. (1986). Staff development and the process of teacher change. *Educational Researcher, 15*, 5–12.

Hunter, M. (1990). *Discipline that develops self-discipline.* El Segundo, CA: Tip Publications.

Lysiak, Fae. (1985). *Time on task: Time utilization, 1984–1985.* Fort Worth, TX: Fort Worth Independent School District, Texas Department of Research and Evaluation.

14

Examples: Accelerant or Deterrent to Learning?

"Give me an example" is a familiar request when one does not understand. Only recently, however, have we become aware of the potential of an example to activate the power of using something the student has already learned to facilitate new learning. Examples from the students' own experience also accelerate students' ability to generate meaning for new learning. Building connections in the student's brain makes the learner an active participant in the processing of new material.

Transfer of Learning

We have long known that past learnings can transfer either positively (assisting) or negatively (interfering) with the acquisition of new learning. For example, knowing how to steer a car will positively transfer and assist with learning to steer a truck. That same knowledge, however, can transfer negatively and cause problems when steering a boat, because the immediate steering response of cars is not the same as the delayed steering response of boats, and a "wake like a corkscrew" can be the result.

Skilled teachers "hook into" past learnings so that students can apply those understandings that assist acquisition of new learning. It is equally important that old learnings that might interfere with new learning *not* be activated in the student's brain. We don't want students to see the French word *robe* before they hear and pronounce the word using the French *r*. If they see *robe*, their natural tendency to pronounce the word with the English *r* might interfere with or slow down learning the French pronunciation (negative transfer). Once students have learned the French pronunciation, however, seeing the word can positively transfer old learning to help them remember that *robe* means "dress."

Merlin Wittrock's generative theory of learning stipulates that the generation of meaning will be stimulated by a teacher's use of examples that connect appropriate elements of what a student already knows

Examples may be perceived directly or recalled from students' long-term memory.

to relevant aspects of what is to be learned. The consequences of teaching can only be understood as a function of what the teaching stimulates the student to do with the material.

Effective Examples

If the teacher's examples have certain critical characteristics, positive transfer will more predictably occur, and learning will be accelerated. If those characteristics are not present, examples (no matter how vivid, humorous, or well-intended) have high probability of producing negative transfer, thereby, making the new learning more difficult for the student.

Because examples are such a powerful way of hooking into past learning, teachers need to know the critical attributes or characteristics of an effective example so that they can better generate or select examples, check them for their effective potential, and then use them for the maximum benefit of students.

Producing Effective Examples

To generate or to select examples and then validate effective examples, a teacher needs to do the following:

1. Identify the "Essence" of What Is to Be Learned
In order to select or generate an effective example, the teacher needs to identify the "essence" or critical attributes of the concept, skill, or generalization to be learned: the elements on which the student is to focus attention. A critical attribute is that which makes something what it is; no other thing has that particular attribute or set of attributes.

Examples of Critical Attributes

- Mammals possess mammary glands and hair.
- A restrictive clause restricts the word that it modifies to a particular instance.
- *Persevere* means to make oneself continue doing something even though one is tempted to stop.
- A pledge is a verbal statement (written or oral) made to convince someone else that the pledger intends to do something.

2. Use Examples From the Student's Own Experience
A student cannot generate meaning (understand what the language is intended to convey) when there is no source for that meaning in the stu-

dent's past knowledge or experience (long-term memory). Consequently, any example used must reflect something the student already knows or has experienced.

Examples

- For a student in Alaska, a seal might be a more meaningful mammal than a cow.
- For students who enjoyed fishing, "The huge fish that I caught yesterday" might exemplify a meaningful restrictive clause.
- For most students, making oneself finish one's homework would be more meaningful for the understanding of *persevere* than would exercising every day.
- To pledge to come in from recess on time every day could be more meaningful than pledging to clean the yard.

3. Check the Examples for Ambiguity
Once the critical attribute has been identified, an example that highlights the attribute without ambiguous or confusing elements needs to be generated or selected first by the teacher and later by students.

Examples

- Mammal: "A cow is a mammal." Whales also are mammals, but their living in water like fish can confuse the issue so they should not be used as a beginning example.
- "A robin or a sparrow is a bird." Don't introduce a penguin or ostrich at first.
- To say "The color of the book was red" leaves no question of the meaning of the last word. To say "The book was red" could cause confusion of *red* with *read*.

4. Avoid Emotional or Controversial Overtones
An effective example is relevant and interesting, but it is not loaded with emotion or controversy that could distract the student's attention from the critical attribute. The following examples have emotional distractors.

Examples

- "Whales are mammals that are in danger of extinction."
- "Let's develop a restrictive clause for the subject 'communists.'"

- "You should be ashamed if you have not persevered."
- "Should you ever make a pledge that you don't intend to keep?"

In the above examples, students are tempted to think of something that will distract them from the concept being learned.

Tips for Presenting Effective Examples

Highlight Critical Attributes by Obvious "Nonexemplars"

For examples that "exemplify" the critical attributes, the following techniques will make them increasingly effective. Half of knowing what something is, is knowing what it is not. Sometimes a teacher can make more vivid the critical attribute of the concept, skill, or understanding to be attained by using "nonexemplars," which are similar but obviously do not possess the critical attribute. Nonexemplars, just like examples that illustrate, should avoid the contamination of emotions and ambiguity. They should enable the student to see the difference between the example and nonexemplar.

Examples

Restrictive Clause: In "The boy who is my best friend was hurt," the clause indicates the specific boy and is restrictive. In "A boy, who wore a school T-shirt, was hurt," the clause doesn't restrict the information to a particular boy; it gives additional information and is nonrestrictive.

Persevere: "Tom persevered. He made himself finish his homework before he turned on his favorite television program" makes it clear that no one else forced Tom to finish and that he would have preferred to watch TV. "Tom loved the assignment and finished it before dinner" is not an example of perseverance because he had no desire to stop.

Pledge: To convince the teacher she really meant it, Ruth said, "I pledge three hours of my time each week to the tutorial program." "I'll do some tutoring" may or may not be a pledge.

Analyze Each Example in Advance

An example is more likely to be effective if it is carefully thought out in advance by the teacher. Thinking "on your seat" is easier than thinking "on your feet." Occasionally, a burst of brilliance occurs while teaching and a superb example surfaces. Most effective examples, however, are the outcome of a painstaking search followed by examination and validation of that example in terms of the four criteria that have been described.

Introduce Teacher-Generated Examples First

To ensure "quality control" of the example, the teacher should give most, if not all, of the examples at the beginning of new learning. An incorrect or imprecise student example can cause a great deal of interference with the clarity and success of other students' learning. Unless the teacher has checked student-generated examples in advance, those are better left until later in learning, when the purpose is to validate and extend students' understanding by having them generate additional examples.

Analyzing Effective Examples

Common Fraction Example

The following is an example of how a teacher might generate examples before teaching common fractions, a content area frequently frustrating to students.

1. *Essence:* The critical attribute is that fractions express a ratio between equivalent parts to the whole.

2. Manipulatives and valid examples from the student's own experience: equivalent parts of pizzas, a candy bar divided in squares, graph paper all qualify because—

   a. Parts are equal

   b. Within the student's past experience

   c. Contain no ambiguity or emotional overtones (unless it is just before lunch)

3. Invalid examples of fractions (Don't use them!)

   a. *Missing critical attribute:* "Fractions are things cut into parts." The concept of *equivalent* parts is critical. Pies are a commonly used example but usually they are not cut into equal parts at home (some get a big piece, others a sliver). Pizzas, on the other hand, usually are cut into equivalent parts.

   b. *Ambiguity and emotional overtones:* "One half of all murders are premeditated." In this example, students are distracted by the emotional overtones of murderers and by the more complex concept of a fraction of a group of individual instances. Part of a group is a much more difficult concept than one obvious whole cut into equivalent parts. Also, a part of a group is not so directly in students' visual experience as pizzas and candy bars for which there is visual memory to assist in the beginning of attaining the concept of fractions. A group should be used later because parts of a group also are essential to understanding fractions.

    c. *Examples that may confuse with complexity:* "I have only a fraction of my work done." While this is technically correct, to most students it merely means, "I've started but not finished." They don't think of it as a part or fraction of a whole that is divided into equivalent parts.

Concrete manipulatives frequently are used for initial instruction of fractions so that students generate for themselves the relation of equal parts to the whole. Later, a teacher can use verbal examples: like all good examples, these should embody the characteristics of highlighting the essence of the concept, be in the students' knowledge or experience, be unambiguous and have no emotional distractors.

Definition of "Courage" Example

Sometimes it is not possible to concretize an example, and verbal examples need to be used. In this case, the teacher must take special precautions so that the examples contribute to, rather than muddy, students' understanding. The following examples might be used for the concept of "courage."

1. *Essence:* The person experiences fear or knowledge of the risk involved, but proceeds anyway.
2. Valid examples
   a. "If you fear giving a report in front of group but you volunteer to be first, you are behaving courageously."
   b. "If you are afraid of being rebuffed by going up to a new student and introducing yourself but you make yourself do it, you are behaving courageously."
   c. "The astronauts knew that if things went wrong, they never would return to earth, so they were courageous when they first went into outer space."
3. Invalid examples of courage
   a. *Missing critical attribute:*
      • "Think of something you are afraid to do and of someone who is courageous enough to do it." The person who does it may have no fear: accomplished public speakers, skilled salespeople, experienced flyers.
      • "Lion trainers are courageous." Although there is danger involved, most lion trainers are no more afraid than are experienced drivers on a congested freeway, where there is much more chance of an accident.

b. *Ambiguity or emotional overtones:* "Suppose in the middle of the night you heard a noise that sounded like a burglar was trying to get in your window, what would you do?" Such a question invites fear from some students, bravado from others. Also solutions have high probability of distracting students' attention from the concept of courage and focusing

Eventually, students should constuct their own examples to demonstrate comprehension.

them on inventing actions, which is not the intent of the example.

c. *Examples that may confuse with complexity:* "How sure do you think Columbus was that the world was round? If he was really sure, he was not courageous. Was he courageous if he was pretty sure but not really sure?" This introduces the notions of probability and that fear exists on a continuum. While, this may be an excellent discussion topic later, it does not belong in the introduction of the concept of courage.

Conclusion

The use of examples is a deceptively simple teaching technique. Every teacher uses examples but sometimes not as productively as is now known to be possible. Generating valid examples is a rigorous test of basic understanding of what is being taught. Generating interesting or humorous examples that use students' past knowledge and highlight the essence or critical attribute without ambiguous or emotional overtones is a manifestation of artistry in teaching.

Bibliography

Craik, F. I. M. (1979). Human memory. *Annual Review of Psychology, 30*, 63–102.

15

Making Material
Meaningful

Memorizing definitions or rules with no meaning such as "Yours is not to reason why, just invert and multiply" unfortunately has become symptomatic of how too many students process content. The cause seems to be a national focus on getting the right answer quickly, rather than understanding what one is doing. This educational ailment is being perpetuated by teachers who were victims of that "right answer" system and by achievement tests that require selection of the correct answer rather than the understanding that leads to future problem solving.

Meaning that is generated by students is one of our most essential and powerful accelerants to learning. Meaning does not exist in material, but exists in the relationship of the material to be learned to the student's already acquired knowledge and experience: what already is in the student's brain. When students actively make connections between what is to be learned and what they already know, they are generating meaning. M. C. Wittrock's generative theory of learning maintains that learners must generate or construct meaning for themselves; no one can do it for them, but excellent teaching helps them accomplish this cognitive feat. Students' ability to generate meaning can be immeasurably increased by teachers' decisions that focus on the importance of meaning and on ways to teach the student to generate that meaning.

In addition, teachers can contribute to students' "intuitive feeling" for a subject. This is a highly desirable attribute that results in learning becoming easier. One important assist to students is teaching for processing by both left and right hemispheres. Unfortunately, too many students are trying to follow the left hemisphere, linear, mumbo-jumbo of meaningless rules: "When subjects are jointed by *or*, the subject closest to the verb determines the verb form" or "Cross out the 9, make it an 8, put a 1 in front of the 6, and subtract" or "Osmosis is the flow of liquid through a membrane from the liquid of the lesser density to the liquid of the greater density."

Although the examples in this chapter are focused primarily on simple math examples, variations on the same techniques should be applied to social studies, language arts, economics, geography, history, science, or voctech classes. In every content area, basic concepts and vocabulary need to be understood. Also, sophistication with quantitative relationships is important to dealing productively with all content. One is always working with probability, ratios, relationships, and time sequence. The professional techniques described in this chapter can be used to assist all students to generate meaning.

Most educators acknowledge that acquisition of many concepts and generalizations should begin with visual and concrete manipulations. For example, students can "right hemispherically see" and concretely experience what is meant when two pennies are put with three pennies to create a set of five pennies. From the concrete, students can move to the increasingly abstract, representational (circles or pictures of pennies: 00 + 000) and symbolic (Xs or slashes: XX + XXX) to completely abstract concepts ($2 + 3 = 5$), which can generalize to any situation. This move from "concrete and personally meaningful to generalized abstractions" is true in any context.

It is possible, however, for the "abstract" to float up into pure abstraction and lose all connection with the real world if students perform the chore of merely memorizing more difficult combinations and algorithms, with absolutely no connection to anything meaningful.

By the time students have "fogged through" multiplication and division and then tackled common fractions, all semblance of meaning may have vanished and a nation of "mathaphobes" (or "languagephobes" or "sciencephobes") is the result. Any generalization, whether it is related to numbers, literature, social problems, or whatever, needs to be associated with meaning in real life to enable students to generate their own meaning as they work with symbols and abstractions.

How can we reverse this undesirable trend of meaningless content and contribute to students who understand, enjoy, and find content useful in their daily dealings with the world: from personal budgets to national debt, from local geography to outer space, from playing games to statistical relationships, from personal economics to national trends? While there is no quick panacea, the following techniques will go far toward accomplishing this objective. Examples cited in this chapter are deliberately simple so all readers will follow them. Teachers of more advanced content should extrapolate to their own more complex situations.

Techniques for Generating Meaning

1. First, teachers must test their own understanding of whatever concept they are teaching by generating problems that embody the concept and that are relevant to the lives of the particular students being taught. (See chapter 14 for a fuller discussion of examples.) Textbook examples such as "Farmer John and his peck of apples" won't do, unless you're in an area that produces apples. A teacher's examples should reflect students' current interests and activities: "If the cost of hamburgers in our cafeteria increased to _____."

2. Each day's learning opportunity should be introduced with a situation that relates today's lesson to a student's immediate daily life. Money, TV, games, and food have universal interests. However, students' interests will vary with age, locale, customs, and current activities, so the problems used should reflect those interests. Because we can't include examples for all content, again we will use math.

Examples
- If your mother put 2 chocolate chip cookies in your lunch and your dad didn't know she had done this so he put 2 more chocolate chip cookies in your lunch, when you opened your lunch, how many chocolate chip cookies would you have to eat or to share with your friend?
- If 50-cent desserts were reduced to 40 cents and you bought 6 for your family, how much money would you need to pay for them?

- If your pizza was cut into 8 equal pieces and you gave half to your friend, how many eighths of a pizza would be left for you to eat?
- Suppose there were a 25% discount on all motorcycles and you wanted one that, before the discount, cost $_____. How much money would you need to buy it?
- If you worked to increase your speed by 15% when you did homework, how much time would you be saving each hour?

After numbers have been connected with reality, it is all right to practice computing to develop speed and accuracy. Periodically, however, that computation should be reconnected to meaning.

   3.   *Students should be encouraged to generate (construct) their own meaning by generating examples from their own lives and explaining in their own words (paraphrasing) the concepts and generalizations they are learning.* If students cannot generate a word problem from their own lives that will fit the numbers in the assigned problem, they don't really understand what they are doing. There may be exceptions if students work with *very* advanced concepts. Here too, however, often there are real-life applications.

Examples
- $27 \times 21 =$ "If I had 27 goldfish in my tank and they each laid 21 eggs that all hatched, how many baby goldfish would I then have?"
- $2/3 \div 1/2 =$ "If I had 2/3 of an hour and it took 1/2 hour to mow one lawn, how many lawns could I mow?"
- $2X + 30 = 80$ "If I bought two pair of the same jeans and 30 dollars' worth of T-shirts and my bill was $80, how much would each pair of jeans cost?"

Making real-life situations fit symbols is not a feat most students (or teachers) accomplish with ease at first. Both are so accustomed to functioning according to memorized procedures, without any personal meaning, that initially it may be difficult for them to assign real significance to their learning and practice.

Problems can be based on reality or fantasy ("If I could fly to Mars"), but they should not be a distortion of reality. An example such as "If I ate 27 apples and then ate 40 more" only contributes to "it ain't never happened."

   4.   *Usually students should be able to visually represent their understanding to show they comprehend what they are doing.* This visual display could take the form of an outline, a map, graph, Venn diagram, or picture. Such a representation aims at having students use right hemisphere processing.

Examples:

If 3 dogs get two bones each, how many bones would you need for all 3 dogs?

If you got a 20% discount and the book originally cost $10, how much would you need to pay?

you pay

you don't pay

If you had 2/3 of a pie and your family needed 1/2 of the pie per meal, for how many meals would you have enough pie?

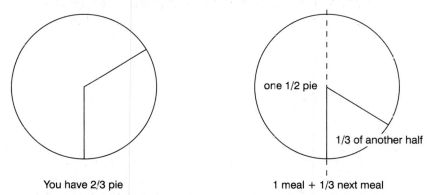

You have 2/3 pie   1 meal + 1/3 next meal

5. *Students should be able to diagnose the parts of a particular process, concept, or generalization they understand and the parts they don't.* As a result, they should become increasingly responsible for their own content literacy, asking questions that link the subject with their own experience and creating the kind of practice work they need in order to develop fluency with each concept. When students ask, "How did you get this?" or "Why do you do that?," you know they are becoming responsible for their own learning. "I thought the answer of $1\frac{1}{3}$ meant $1\frac{1}{3}$ pies. Now I see it means $1\frac{1}{3}$ *half* pies. It's hard to remember that the answer means that many of the quantity or set you're dividing it by."

6.   *Students need to be able to set up situations, experiments, or equations, using relevant information to answer the question posed, and then estimate the reasonableness of their answer.* While the hand calculator or computer has eliminated the former necessity for speed in calculation of more complex problems, knowledge of number facts is the foundation for the critical skill of estimation and for the monitoring of calculator accuracy. Therefore, a great deal of practice in estimating answers and judging the reasonableness of an answer needs to be provided. This also is true in other content areas where one is using reference material. Judgments need to be made as to the authenticity of the information and the accuracy of the conclusion.

Examples

- Suppose tapes were on sale for less than $5.00 including tax. You wanted to buy 7 of them. If you had $34.95, would you have enough money for the tapes you wanted?

- If you buy 8 items that, with tax, cost less than 75 cents, will $5.95 be enough to pay for your purchases?

- If an item costs between $2.00 and $3.00, how much money had you better save in order to be sure to have enough to buy 9 of them?

Similar judgments about selecting references, the authenticity of sources, the validity of conclusions must be made in every content area.

Conclusion

To assist students to automate the basics of any subject is similar to learning the facts in order to do simple computation and to estimate. A teacher's knowledge of practice theory will suggest a student (1) work on small meaningful amounts (3-10 facts), (2) in short intense practice periods (3-10 minutes, not a half hour), (3) mass that practice at the beginning (several short, intense practice periods scheduled close together) that produces fast learning, (4) then distribute the practice (spacing practice periods with longer and longer times between them) for long retention, and (5) then consistently be provided with knowledge of results so performance steadily improves.

Any content area can become relevant and meaningful to students. Until students get into very abstract material, concepts to be learned can be demonstrated and concretized in a way that relates to every student's experience. As we make learning personally meaningful, instead of its being a meaningless, memorized ritual with rules, we can reverse the trend of confusion and avoidance that has become the hallmark of many classes. The future of students who possess content literacy is bright—*if* we make it so by our teaching.

Bibliography

Hunter, M. (1969.) *Teach more—faster*. El Segundo, CA: Tip
    Publications.

Wittrock, M. C. (1986). Education and recent research on attention
    and knowledge acquisition. In S. L. Friedman, K. A. Klivington,
    & R. W. Peterson (Eds.), *The brain, cognition, and education.*
    New York: Academic Press.

Wittrock, M. C. (1990). Processes of comprehension. *Educational
    Psychologist, 24*, 345–376.

c h a p t e r

16

Helping Students
Automate Basic
Skills[1]

One important basis of every student's success in school and in life resides in the ability to use basic skills automatically, routinely working with words and with quantitative relationships. Skill in application of these two areas of learning to new situations is necessary not only in preparing for a satisfying job or in fashioning a career, but also in productively participating in our society. To be inept with words and in the understanding of numerical relationships is to miss out on

[1]Some of the content of this chapter originally appeared in *Here's How*, NAESP, September 1987.

185

important parts of being a whole person since so much other knowledge depends on the two basic understandings.

Helping Students Increase Vocabulary

In our society, so much information is conveyed by language that a student with an extensive vocabulary has a distinct learning advantage. Knowing the meaning of words is one of the most enabling learning competencies students can possess, and one of the best predictors of success at any level of education. When teachers (and parents) help students develop accurate meanings for words, they are making a major contribution to students' academic progress. Meaning, however, does not exist in the material (words) being learned. Rather, meaning (the information being conveyed) has to be generated by the student through developing a relationship between the new material and what the student already knows or has experienced: what is in long-term memory. Consequently, teachers and/or parents can creatively use the following procedures so that students can acquire new vocabulary more easily, generate accurate meanings for words, and transfer knowledge of words more accurately and efficiently to new contexts.

   1.   Introduce the new word with an example from the student's own life. To help students extend their functional vocabulary, by their generating meanings for words new to them, those words need to be introduced in a context meaningful to the student. In this way, new words are related to what the student does, or thinks about, or remembers.

   Example
   "*Peruse* means you examine something and consider it with attention and in detail. John *perused* the directions for the word processor so that he could use it to produce and edit the script he wrote for our class play. That means he read the directions carefully and paid attention to every detail that was explained in the directions. Marge *perused* that chapter in our social studies book so that she could help John with the dialogue in his script. Then all the details of the characters' lines would be accurate. All of you *perused* the newspaper articles so that you knew about current events and you could answer any questions your classmates asked. If you had just skimmed through your articles and paid no attention to detail, you would not have perused them." (Note, many people inaccurately think that *peruse* means "to skim," which is not its meaning.)

Of course, students have to generate their own meaning. It can't be "just told by the teacher," but by giving these kinds of examples, the teacher *increases* the probability that students generate accurate meaning and make the vocabulary their own.

Giving several (three to five) examples that reflect *varied* occurrences in students' daily lives helps students generate accurate understanding of the meaning of words. Once students understand, giving examples of similar situations that illustrate what particular words do *not* mean also helps the student learn correct rather than incorrect usage.

Example

"When people say you are *considerate*, they mean that you consider or think about what another person feels or would like to do and you try to accommodate the other person's needs or desires. You were *considerate* when you knew a relative wanted to talk to you about what your class is studying, and you stayed and told your relative what you were doing at school, although you wanted to do something else. A father was *considerate* of his son and his son's friends when he knew they wanted to watch a cartoon on TV, and he wanted to listen to the news; but he let his son and his friends watch the cartoon. A daughter was *considerate* of her father when she saw that he was tired, so she didn't hold him to their plans for going shopping. If she also did not want to go shopping, that would not be showing consideration."

Students need to learn how to look up words in the dictionary; however, the words assigned should be in context. Context gives words different meanings. Copying or memorizing definitions is *not* the most efficient and effective way of extending students' vocabularies, unless the meaning of those words is translated by students into sentences about their everyday experiences.

2. Check students' comprehension. To check on whether students really understand the meaning of a particular word (whether that meaning comes from you or from the dictionary) and to help them make that word a usable and permanent part of their speaking and writing vocabularies, the teacher should have students practice using that word in several "meaning loaded" sentences about themselves. A meaning-loaded sentence is one in which the meaning of the word can be inferred from the sentence. "I was tired and wanted to quit, but I made myself keep on working; I *persevered*."

3. Work on only three to five words at a time. Students should work on learning only a few new words at a time, usually not more than five, fewer with younger students, certainly not a vocabulary list of 10 or 20 words at one time. When students work on only a few words and use them in sentences loaded with meaning for them, the odds are very good that students will learn the words, store them in long-term memory, recall them when needed, and have increased their capacity to express themselves and to understand what others mean. When students know and can use those first few words, they can work on the next five on the list. Systematically, they should go back to review words already learned so that those words are "automated" or internalized and will be used in subsequent speaking and writing. Teachers need to encourage this technique so that students' vocabularies continue to expand.

Of course, becoming proficient in language skills—whether it be reading, writing, speaking, or listening—involves much more than vocabulary development. Still, words are at the core of all language and thinking, essential in the development of concepts and generalizations, which are expressed in words, plus the discriminations that tell us when those generalizations are or are not appropriate to a particular situation.

4.   *Have students keep a record of new words that have been learned in individual word lists with meaning-loaded sentences.* Such a list is encouraging to students because they can see how many new words they have acquired. It also reminds them of words they may not have used recently and may need to review. Have them select, from their reading and listening, additional words that intrigue them. After words are learned and can be used in meaningful sentences, give students the opportunity to teach "their words" to other students as well as to learn other students' words. It is amazing how such activities result in promoting students' zest for words, with resultant acceleration in processing language.

In every case, teachers or parents who plan for the acceleration of students' learning of concepts and generalizations through extension of vocabulary will find that the four procedures just described bring increased student competence to the learning process. Using the procedures, student can truly internalize what they have learned and transfer it to new situations.

Helping Students Use Basic Skills Automatically

Knowing information, processes, and procedures so well that they can be applied automatically—that is without requiring very much of the brain's neural energy—releases that energy for dealing with more complex material and situations. As an example, developing automatic reading skills enables the reader to get information quickly, which then can be used for more demanding tasks.

The process of developing automaticity is basically the same for information, processes, and procedures whether they be solving equations, conducting an experiment to isolate variables, applying a procedure or a formula, analyzing a chapter, learning number facts, or any other skill that makes more complex tasks possible. Important basic skills need to be taught in such a way that they become personally meaningful to students as well as automatic.

To examine the process of developing automaticity, we will begin with a very simple example. Learning basic facts in addition, subtraction, multiplication, and division was a chore for many of us and continues to be a chore for many students today, even though those facts are critically important to functioning successfully in our society. While a great deal of computation now is done with a calculator, knowing number facts still is essential to estimating the correctness of the machine-produced answers, to doing simple problems in our heads, and to escaping total enslavement by dependence on the presence of a machine. Moreover, the process of learning and automating facts in any content area can be made a great deal easier, more meaningful, and can produce increased transfer to subsequent life situations if the teacher (or, for that matter, parents) creatively develops the following procedures. We will describe the general procedures for practice sessions, using specific examples relating to practicing simple math facts.

1.   Start each practice with a meaningful example from the student's own life. For learning addition facts, an example of such an approach might be this: "If you had 5 pennies in your pocket and I gave you 2 more pennies, how many pennies would you have?" For learning multiplication facts: "If hamburgers were on sale for 95 cents each and you bought 3 of them, how much money would you need to pay for them?" For subtraction facts: "If you had 17 cents and you bought a balloon for 9 cents, how much money would you have left to buy something else?" For division facts: "If you had 63 trading cards to divide equally among 7 friends, how many would each get?"

Make each example come from that student's personal, everyday experience. *Meaning* can be defined as the student's generating *relationships* between new learning and what s/he already knows or has experienced. In this way, new learning becomes connected with what exists in the student's long-term memory, and thus becomes easier to grasp.

To test whether number combinations are meaningful to particular students, ask them to create a situation from their own experience that will go with one of the facts to be learned. If the class is working on 9 plus 7, the student should be able to make up a real-life situation such as this: "If I did 9 problems in the morning and 7 problems in the afternoon, I would have done 16 problems." For 45 divided by 9, "If I had to read 45 pages and I read 9 each night, it would take me 5 nights to finish."

The same procedures can be applied to more complex learnings to give them meaning. Here are some examples: "X^2 could mean that you receive the same number of dollars per hour as the number of hours you work. X is a variable. Its value varies. If you work 5 hours you will earn $5 per hour. If you work 8 hours, you will make $8 per hour." "Let's look at the results of whether or not you do your homework. It could affect whether or not you have the skills to get the job you want (or whether or not you win the game)." "If you were analyzing your day, what are some ways you could categorize (group) what happened?"

2.   *Select three to five facts that the student has not yet learned and practice only those—in short intense practice periods.* If remembering five facts proves difficult for a student, work on only three (6 x 3, 6 x 4, 6 x 5), working in a context familiar to the student. If remembering is easy for a student, work on five, not more even though you are tempted. This close repetition is called "massed practice" and means that once meaning has been generated, the student goes over the same small group of facts several times in a few minutes.

These facts could be in history, geography, science, economics, or literature. With more complicated learnings, it may be difficult to think of varied situations where the same information, process, or procedure can be applied several times. It is essential, however, that students "mass practice" what they have just learned in as wide a variety of situations as possible, to more nearly ensure the transfer of that learning to future situations where it is appropriate. When the student can give reasonably fast answers to questions involving these facts (randomly presented—not in order), the facts should be mixed with ones the student already knows (6 x 5, 6 x 1, 6 x 4, 6 x 2, 6 x 5, 6 x 4, 6 x 1, 6 x 3). *Then stop!* Several short, intense practice periods of a few minutes will produce more learning than will a long practice period. Also, the student is less likely to become fidgety, to stop thinking, or to object. At the beginning of learning new basic facts or processes, these short practice periods should be scheduled two or three times a day (possibly with students working with a friend), with addition of new facts only as students master the ones being practiced. Already-learned facts occasionally should be mixed in with new ones so that the older ones are reviewed and "stay with" the student (6 x 6, 6 x 7, 6 x 8, then 6 x 5, 6 x 8, 6 x 4, 6 x 9, 6 x 7, 6 x 5).

3.   *Occasionally, go back to formerly learned facts, principles, or procedures.* This is called "distributed" practice, and such occasional review is essential in helping students remember things they previously have learned. By periodic reviews, any skills that have slipped out of the student's memory will be identified so that in subsequent massed practice sessions the student can concentrate on those things forgotten, rehearsing them, then mixing them with the new material being learned—with the result that all information, processes, and procedures get the practice necessary for easy recall and automaticity.

4. *Keep track of what has been learned, in the context of the activities requiring it, on a student's private, individual chart.* In this way, teacher and student (not others, unless the student chooses to show it) can see progress and know what has been accomplished and what needs to be reviewed or learned next. Such a record will also help the teacher and the student go over older material for distributed practice so it becomes automatic.

If the practice activities are performed for a few minutes at a time, perhaps after breaks, or when the class is assembling, or when an assignment has been completed and a little free time is available, or just before class is dismissed or for homework, students are in for a very pleasant surprise. They will discover how wonderfully painless and efficient the process of automating learning can become.

An important educational goal is to teach students to follow the procedures by themselves, on their own, so that they can become self-directed learners and practice anything they want to remember during times when they are engaged in activities that really do not require them to think—doing dishes, riding in a car, or waiting at the doctor's office, for a bus, or in a checkout line. Students should be encouraged to metacognate (to monitor their own learning) in order to make this "learning and remembering" process so routine in their lives that they automatically use "nonthinking" time for automating learning—doing their own distributed practice. When they assume that responsibility, the teacher will not need to encroach upon precious recreation time and subject a resentful student to more homework drill.

These techniques for automating learnings that need high-speed recall and that are needed for more complex tasks are not meant to suggest that automating basic facts is the ultimate goal of instruction. Obviously, to become effective in thinking and solving problems, the student must be able to perform more complex tasks like these: identify the question being asked; identify what the answer will signify; select the cognitive operation required; determine or create categories; set up the problem, solve it, and determine if the answer is reasonable. The ability to evaluate the solution, which rests on the ability to think analytically, is essential to efficient and accurate problem solving.

All of these skills also are more efficiently and effectively achieved if teachers—

- Begin with examples that have meaning in the student's own life
- Pace students so they work on only a few skills or concepts at a time
- Mass and then distribute practice
- Make accomplishment visible to the student

17

Helping a Student Who Is "Stuck"

One important skill that needs to be in the repertoire of a professional educator is how to give effective help to students who are having difficulty on a task. This chapter outlines some general points to consider in everyday classroom practice.

Students need to feel in charge of the help a teacher gives. Unsolicited assistance from the teacher can make students feel they are judged to be incapable of doing the task by themselves. This does not mean you do not help a student whom you know needs help. You simply need to be careful how you do it. You can encourage students' feelings of being responsible and competent if you first watch to see what the student is doing or ask him/her to tell you exactly what s/he is trying to do. Then you might ask:

- "What have you done so far?"
- "What are you supposed to do next?"
- "What part of it do you understand?"
- "What part is not clear?"

If the student is doing the process correctly but is not yet secure, DON'T show him/her a new method or "an easier way" or "the way you learned it in school" or a "shortcut." (Something being learned must be fully understood before an additional way is introduced, or none of it will be learned effectively.)

When you find out just where the student is "stuck," ask a question that focuses on the clue that will enable the student to take the next step him/herself. If s/he still is stuck, ask a simpler question that narrows the student's focus. Keep narrowing your questions until s/he is able to see what to do.

Examples

- In a word problem, "Are you combining or separating quantities?" "What tells you the operation to use?" "What quantities are you combining?"
- In an outline, "What might be some categories?"
- To answer a question, "What information do you have that might help (is relevant)?"
- For writing, "What information do you think is important for the reader?"
- For a reading report, "What part is most interesting to you?"
- For a spelling word, "How would you spell the first part?" "What letter is at the beginning?" Obviously if the word is nonphonetic, you should supply the spelling, rather than having the students guess.
- For punctuation, "What is the rule about _____?" "How could you use it in this sentence?"
- In figuring out directions, "What does this part tell you to do?" "What does the next part say?"
- Simplify the task to one for which the student already knows the answer and help him/her figure out how s/he got it, "How would you do this (simpler) example of 50% of 6?" "What oper-

ation using 5 and 6 would give you a 3? Then what would you do to get the answer to 63% of 97?"

Such questions focus the student on important aspects but leave him/her with feelings of competence rather than dependence. Obviously, if the student lacks necessary information, the teacher should supply the answer to the question. Students cannot generate that which is not in their brains. Guessing, without information, only produces more confusion.

At times, you may need to demonstrate the process while telling the student what is going on in your mind, what you are looking at, the cues you are using that tell you what to do next. This helps the student learn the mental process that precedes action. Then, observe while the student does the activity, helping if indicated with questions that direct attention to the relevant features. "I am thinking, Does 'the captain of our Football Team' mean the same person as 'Bill Barns'? If so, it is an appositive, and I set it off with commas. You do the next one and say what you're thinking."

When s/he does it correctly, decide whether you should (1) move away and let the student continue or (2) stay and guide the student through one or two similar examples until you feel s/he can do it alone.

Watch out for the student who exploits your help to keep from working or who enjoys dependency. Don't stay too long with one student. If you feel a student needs a great deal of time and help, check the assignment to see if it is appropriate for that student's stage of learning.

Always reinforce effort and compliment growth rather than waiting for perfect performance. "That's coming." "Now you're getting it." "You're really trying, so pretty soon it will be easier." "Some people would get discouraged, but you really stick to it. That's great!"

The way you help a student can significantly contribute to students' self-direction and achievement with resultant increase of students' self-esteem and feelings of competency to "figure it out and do it myself."

18

Putting the Student ("You") at the Center of Learning

One of the most ubiquitous words in teaching is *I*. "*I* want you to turn to (look at, underline, do, consider, be ready to, line up, turn in)." "*I* like the way ____." "Now, the next thing *I* have planned is ____." "*I* am going to ____." We have become an *I, I, I'ing* profession.

You is the power word. Consider the difference between "*I* am going to have you ____" and "Now *you* are ready to ____." *You* places power and confidence in the student. *I* maintains teacher control. (Yes, in the past, teachers were told to make *I* statements, but we've learned a lot since then. In the past, steak was a staple in a reducing diet, but we've also learned better than that.)

197

"Open your book to page 32, read the first paragraph, and be ready to state what you think the story will be about" expresses confidence in the student's ability to direct self. "Now *I'm* going to ask you to turn to page 32. *I* want you to read the first paragraph and be ready to tell *me* what the story is about" implies that the teacher is the controlling agent in the student's learning.

An especially seductive use of *I* is a statement of approval. "I like the way you're listening (working, raising hands, lining up, writing)." That implies, "You're pleasing me and when you don't, I won't like you." It also suggests that it is the student's job to please me (and it is not!).

You statements build students' self-esteem. When a person feels that his/her effort and ability produced excellence, self-esteem is enhanced and effort will increase. "You look great in that outfit. You certainly have good taste in clothes" gives a very different message from "I like your outfit." "You did an excellent job of using descriptive words in your story. The reader could really hear and see what you meant" is infinitely more powerful than "I was impressed by your use of descriptive words." A *you* statement attributes success to the student's ability and effort.

The *you* statement requires the teacher to specify why something is acceptable or excellent, which gives more specific "knowledge of results" to the student and enhances the student's ability to identify and repeat that which made a quality performance.

"You are wise to try different ways of writing that, to see which one best states what you mean" encourages a student's effort and the generation and selection of alternatives, plus giving more precise knowledge of what will result in a future successful performance. "I like the way you're working" is infinitely less informative and effective.

When *is* the use of *I* appropriate? When you are giving information about yourself, it is accurate to say, "I like your outfit. It is my favorite color." You'll build more self-esteem and feelings of competence, however, if you elaborate with "That color certainly complements your eyes and makes you look vibrant. It also happens to be my favorite color" or "You did a great job with your surprise ending in the story. Most people never would have guessed it. In fact, I was completely off base."

It is also desirable to eliminate the use of *I*'s in the instructional conference that follows observation in peer coaching and supervision. *You* adds to the power of an observer's feedback. Throw away your "I was impressed by _____," "I liked the way you _____," "I noticed that _____." Replace these *I*'s with "You were effective when _____, because _____," "You successfully _____, when you _____," "You captured students' interest by _____," "You increased the probability of their remembering when you _____."

A valid use of *I* conveys information about the speaker. "I am perplexed by _____," "I don't know the answer to _____," "I was wondering

"You are listening so well, you will do it just right!" should replace, "I like the way you are listening."

if _____"—each of these gives the listener information about something that was occurring in the speaker's mind.

It is not a mortal sin to use *I*. It's simply a habit pattern that we know is not as effective as using *you*. Use an observer or a tape recorder to tally how many *I*'s you're using in teaching. (One teacher used 26 *I*'s in a 20-minute lesson—far more than he had thought.) Once you bring the use of *I* to a conscious level in teaching, coaching, or supervision (most people have said it so many times they're not even aware of it), you can monitor your *I*'s and change most of them to the more powerful *you*'s.

Focusing your eyes and ears on your *I*'s will help you more frequently use the productive, student-enhancing *you*.

Bibliography

Hunter, M., & Barker, G. (1989). Attributed theory and the middle school. *New England League of Middle Schools Journal, 2*(1). P. O. Box 721, Castleton, VT 05735.

Hunter, M., & Barker, G. (1987). If at first. . . .: Attribution theory in the classroom. *Educational Leadership, 45*(4).

19

Repeating Students' Answers: Helpful or Habit?

Repeating students' answers is a practice that has become habitual with some teachers. The reasons given for this repetition may be ones like these:

1. It has been modeled during teachers' previous schooling.
2. It has become an automatic behavior.
3. It is a response that requires no thinking and, therefore, gives the teacher some time to come up with the next question or statement.

4. It is based on a belief that hearing something twice increases learning and retention.

5. It makes students feel good because it validates their answers as correct.

There are times when a student's answer should be repeated, but for *none* of the above reasons.

Valid Reasons for Repeating Answers

Here are some legitimate reasons for repeating answers:

1. *The teacher needs to clarify or extend the answer.*

Examples

• "You're right. *Run* is a verb in this sentence because its function identifies what the boy did. The word *run* doesn't always serve the same function. In a different sentence, *run* could be a noun if it named something such as 'The boy hit a home *run*.'"

• "You were correct when you said you would use 'times,' which means you would multiply, because you're combining equal sets or the same numbers."

Teachers also repeat correct answers if they wish to model and thereby clarify a more accurate grammar form or pronunciation. This is especially valid in a foreign language class or with words whose pronunciation is new or difficult for students.

2. *A second reason for repeating a student's response is to handle an incorrect answer.* The teacher puts the student's answer with the question to which it correctly belongs (dignifying the answer) and then teaches the correct answer to the original question.

Examples

• "Your answer that *run* is a noun would be correct in a sentence where it is the name of something such as 'The home *run* was spectacular.' In your sentence, 'The boy will *run* fast,' *run* refers to the action of the boy, what he will do in the game; therefore, it is a verb."

• "You *could* get the answer by adding. There's a faster way to do it when all the sets, or numbers, are the same or equivalent. What other operation might you use?"

3. *A third reason for repeating the student's answer is to encourage a shy learner.* This repetition should be done with *initial* responses that were not very audible. To ask a student to repeat could result in that student's never again volunteering an answer. Repeating the response confirms that you heard correctly and lets the rest of students know the answer given. Note the word *initial*. If the student continues to answer so softly it is not possible for the rest of the class to hear, some teaching needs to be done.

Examples

- "You're right, *run* is a verb in this sentence."
- "Good thinking, you multiply."

Common Reasons for Repeating Answers

Now, let's examine the most common reasons given for repeating an answer, and learn why such repetition might have an effect opposite to what the teacher intends, which is students' increased learning and feelings of confidence and competence.

1. Repeating has been modeled in previous school experience. Before they knew better, many teachers routinely repeated students' answers. Consequently, teachers may repeat answers because that is what they have observed other teachers do. When something is observed over a period of time, it can become an automatic part of the observer's behavior (gestures, accents, mannerisms, ways of teaching). Observational learning is very powerful and can occur with no intent on the part of the learner to acquire that habit. (See chapter 12.)

2. Repeating answers has become habitual, so teachers often are unaware they are doing it. Many teachers are horrified when they see a videotape or hear an audiotape of their teaching and realize they are repeating almost every answer, when they had no intention of doing so.

3. Repeating an answer gives a teacher time to think of the next question or statement. Repeating an answer serves the same function as "uh-h-h," which fills the silence and gives the speaker time to think of what to say next. Teaching requires high-speed responding, and anything that gives the teacher time to think seems to be desirable. Routinely repeating a student's answer, in most cases, is not a desirable time filler. On the other hand, substituting a few seconds of silence will give the students time to process the information into long-term memory.

4. Hearing something twice facilitates learning and retention. Doing it again (massed practice *by the student*) does increase the speed of initial learning. But hearing it again should be a thoughtful paraphrase of the student's answer by the teacher, not a rote repetition.

An answer that is *not* repeated but is accepted and acted on assures the student that he was right and teaches the others to be attentive.

You would not think of repeating the identical problem or sentence twice in a drill, "5 times 9 equals 45, 5 times 9 equals 45." "Find the verb in the sentence 'The boy will run.' Find the verb in the sentence 'The boy will run.'" Are you convinced that repeating the identical words does not increase learning? Are you convinced that repeating the identical words does not increase learning?

It is important to repeat initial learnings for faster learning and longer retention. The critical attribute, however, is that the student is making a thinking response rather than a repetitive, robotic response. It's much more effective to come back to the same question a few minutes later rather than to have students or teacher repeat it immediately unless there is uncertainty or error in the first response. Returning to a response after a short interval has a much greater impact on learning and retention than does the teacher's rote repetition of the answer.

In psychomotor skills where you are repeating a chain of muscular responses to change discrete responses into a "single production," students' (not the teacher's) repeating a series of responses can be effective. This also is true when a student needs to automate a high-speed cognitive response. In either case, repetition can be overdone.

5. *It makes students "feel good" to have the teacher repeat their answers.* We know of no research or experiential basis for this statement. It does make students feel good to know they are correct, and students need validation of their answers. A much more powerful validation would be "You certainly have been listening carefully—that is correct" or "That was a very insightful answer" or "You must have done very careful thinking to have reached that conclusion." Telling a student that s/he has been perceptive and/or has put forth effort has much more impact than a teacher's robotic repetition.

Placing a student's answer on the board, acknowledging accuracy with a smile, nod, or other gesture gives the same feedback of correctness without repetition of the answer.

Common Results of Repeated Answers

Routinely repeating an answer for any of the above reasons can result in some of the following outcomes, obviously *not* desired by the teacher.

1. *Students learn not to listen to each other, but only to the teacher because s/he is the one who will say what is important or what will be on the test.* We are expending massive efforts to encourage students to listen to each other, learn from each other, and to build on and benefit from others' contributions. The problems of this world are so complex that never again will they be solved by one person, so collaboration is imperative. We have experienced the power of cooperative learning when it is correctly and skillfully done (not poorly done or done by placing groups in charge of their own learning as an abdication of teaching). In such learning, listening is critical.

Listening is one of our most underdeveloped (and important!) skills. We scientifically extinguish that skill when students can anticipate that each answer will be stated twice. In reality, we are teaching students that they don't need to listen; the answer will be given again, so there will be a second chance to hear it.

2. *When teachers repeat answers, shy students learn they don't have to present their ideas so people can hear them.* Those students are given the crutch that someone else will say it for them. Also, when teachers repeat answers, shy students are denied the opportunity to learn to communicate to the group. Encouraging them with "You are absolutely right. Your answer is so important. Say it again so everyone learns it."

Note, we usually *don't* say, "Say it louder so everyone can hear." Emphasis needs to be placed on value and importance, not on decibels.

Most students, given such encouragement, reassurance of correctness, and feeling of the importance of their contribution, will say the answer again with increased volume. A teacher, however, needs to be sensitive to each student's response to the request to say it again and be immediately alert to an overestimation of the student's ability to repeat with more volume. Should the student withdraw, the teacher can quickly intervene with "What I meant was that your answer of _____ (repeating the answer) was so well stated (important, critical to our understanding, insightful) that everyone needs to hear it."

Conclusion

"A negative 6." "A verb." "Multiply." Anyone can repeat an answer. It takes a skilled professional to acknowledge an answer as correct by a response or gesture that builds a student's self-esteem, to respond in a way that corrects errors so the student never loses dignity but learns the correct answer, or to extend or expand a correct answer.

In summary, whether a teacher repeats a student's response depends on that teacher's high-speed metacognition: thinking about or monitoring his/her own professional thinking and decision making while it is occurring.

It is appropriate to repeat an answer if (1) learning will benefit from clarification, extension, or a more correct model; (2) an incorrect answer needs to be corrected and a correct answer prompted; or (3) a shy or hesitant student needs to become more confident and sure of self in order to speak more assertively in the future.

Should none of these three reasons be relevant to particular students and/or situations, a more sophisticated professional decision is being made when a teacher does not routinely repeat students' answers, but expects students to hear, build on, and elaborate on each other's answers.

20

Teaching Students How to Disagree Agreeably

"When everyone thinks the same, not much thinking gets done" is certainly true. Disagreement stimulates thought because a person is encouraged to examine a position, support it, defend it, or modify it on the basis of additional information.

Disagreeing agreeably also is essential to successful cooperative learning, for each member of the cooperative group has responsibility for contributing to mature thinking by the other members. Disagreeing agreeably is a growth-evoking skill that needs to be identified, learned, and practiced in all successful human interactions. It is well worth teachers' and students' time and effort, for it will be useful throughout life.

207

Disagreements, however, if they are disagreeable can cause a person to stop listening and staunchly maintain an unexamined position. This situation of "me against you" is to be avoided for it will produce no intellectual growth, only stubborn hostility. ("It is *too* so!")

To disagree agreeably, one needs to consider the questions:

1. Is the disagreement total or partial? (Usually, there is some degree of agreement, however small, with the other person's point of view.)
2. What information might be supplied to stimulate the other person's reexamination of the situation or problem?

Let's examine both of these questions in detail.

Is the Disagreement Total or Partial?

If we can find some area of agreement with others' points of view and state the conditions under which their views are correct, we align ourselves with them. In this way, we diffuse antagonism without compromising our own beliefs.

Examples

- "It's possible that at times I may have been overconcerned about your performance."
- "There may have been times when you have had more work to do than others."
- "Your candidate (policy, position, assumption, plan, ideas) may have strengths I haven't yet considered."
- "I can understand why you think you're not getting enough allowance when some of your friends are getting more."

By taking a position that is not in direct opposition to the one with which we disagree, we reduce the emotional and verbal tug of war, which only fuels opposition.

The counseling term for this type of response is "fogging." Its purpose is to diffuse the other's adamant position and create a possibility that, with additional information, s/he will "penetrate" the fog surrounding his/her position and modify it to a more clearly defensible one.

There may be a few times, however, in which we completely and totally disagree with the other's position. We can still say so without

Disagreement should generate rethinking and growth rather than hostility.

being disagreeable if we make clear that it is the idea or position with which we disagree, not the person.

Examples

- "And I thought I was being underconcerned about your performance."
- "Our concepts of how much work you do seem to be based on different perceptions and expectations."
- "Our opinions of what is important in a candidate (policy, position, assumption, plan, ideas) must come from different points of view."
- "Our ideas are certainly different. I had the idea your allowance was generous."

How Can Someone Be Encouraged to Reexamine His/Her Position?

We can elicit information to encourage the other person to reexamine his/her position in several ways. We may stimulate such information through questions or give the information directly, or we may encourage the other person to identify it by stating discrepant events that seem to contradict the other person's position. When we are encouraging the other person to reexamine his/her position, it is important that we use a

Learning to challenge and disagree agreeably makes involvement stimulating but enjoyable.

conversational tone of voice, with body language that has no hint of aggression, displeasure, or anger.

Asking a clarifying question elicits specifics from others and lets them know you are open to additional information (which encourages them to be likewise). It also gives you an opportunity to reexamine the basis for your own position—something we all should do.

Here are some examples of questions that clarify the situation.

Examples

- "In which situation do you feel I have been overconcerned?"
- "What work do you feel has not been required of others?"
- "How would you address this situation?"
- "What causes you to feel your allowance should be greater?"

Here are some examples in which the speaker gives direct information to encourage the other person to reconsider his/her position.

Examples

- "You're a very able person, so I'm concerned when you produce work that is not up to your ability."
- "Your work has followed the same pattern as the others."
- "This is what your candidate's published statements (policy, position, assumption, plan, ideas) have been."
- "According to what I can learn, a typical allowance for someone your age is _____."

To *tactfully* point out a discrepancy in the other's reasoning or position can cause that person to move from an absolute position to a conditional one and to be more amenable to a collaborative resolution of the disagreement.

Examples

- "It's not just I, _____ also are concerned about your performance."
- "Your work frequently needs to be redone."
- "Your candidate is not recommended by _____, whom you respect."
- "Tom gets less allowance than you and he's one of your close friends."

Conclusion

The essential element in any agreeable disagreement is to encourage both parties to rethink their positions on the basis of new information or reconsideration of information already possessed. Notice that both persons reconsider; this is not a strategy for winning an argument. As you reconsider and modify or retain your original position on the basis of listening to another's arguments, you become a model for the other person to do likewise. Always to be open to new information or another point of view is the highest level of mature human thinking, dialectical thinking, as you reasonably, responsibly, and respectfully consider the strongest possible argument against your own position. Only when you develop the maturity to do this, can you expect your family, friends, professional associates, students, and nations of the world to do likewise.

Bibliography

Slavin, R. (1990). *Cooperative learning: Theory research and practice.* Englewood Cliffs, NJ: Prentice-Hall.

21

Reducing Paperwork, But Not Instructional Effectiveness

Schools have become nightmares of paperwork: testing, correcting, forms, and bookkeeping for teachers. With the advent of diagnostic-prescriptive teaching and photocopier availability, a blizzard of paper has blinded many educators to more productive ways of engaging students in the learning process, as well as of validating that learning has occurred. As one young teacher lamented, "Having to correct those workbooks every night wrecked my marriage!"

Skilled and creative teachers have discovered productive ways to avoid the paper mill, but for other conscientious teachers who feel they must assign and correct to be on top of stu-

Countless hours are wasted in correcting students' work if the information about students' progress could be secured during class time.

dent learning, this chapter will suggest some ways to accomplish that purpose and still have some sort of life outside of school. Since many of the new techniques described involve different ways for students to respond, the techniques must *taught* to students. Students cannot be expected to use them unless they have learned *how* and had sufficient practice to perform them accurately.

It might also be pointed out that "inspired" ideas of how to implement these techniques in their classrooms can be generated by teachers while they are engaged in routine activities (driving, washing dishes, yard work, cleaning), thereby providing an interesting diversion to monotonous tasks and freeing subsequent time for pursuits that are recreational rather than "wreck-reational." Correcting papers cannot be coupled with routine activities but consumes what otherwise would be well-deserved leisure time.

Diagnosing

Finding out what students know and what they next need to learn is essential to the process of successful instruction. There are three ways to diagnose with minimal paper work involved.

Formal Diagnosis

Formal diagnosis involves a carefully prepared *short* test which, with precision, identifies a specific student's learning accomplishments in a specified, not general, area. General achievement tests do not do this. A well-designed, formal diagnosis is accurate but costly in terms of time needed to design, administer, and correct. Frequently, in such tests, unless they are brief, more data are collected then can be immediately used. Consequently, when an extensive test is used, teachers subsequently may be working from obsolete information that no longer is valid. Therefore, a *short* formal diagnostic test should be given to supply only enough information for immediate use so it can be corrected quickly.

Informal Diagnosis

Observation of students' work and responses (perhaps produced by their "signing" or signaling answers in groups) can be an effective way to informally diagnose. A quick, "rough cut" with not as much precision as formal diagnosis but with reasonable accuracy can identify students' current learnings. Information gathered can be used immediately and students' mistakes corrected as instruction proceeds.

     Students can signal to make responses. For example, punctuation marks can be signaled with hands. A curled index finger makes a comma, an upright index finger makes an exclamation point, two hands can make a question mark, a semicolon, or whatever is needed. With practice, a teacher can learn how to see at a glance that most students know or don't know (what to do with those who know while you're teaching those who don't know is also a professional skill that is possible for all teachers to learn but outside the realm of this chapter).

     Having students make +, -, x, ÷ signs with their fingers are signaled responses that tell if students know which arithmetic operation to use in solving word problems. Students can show a plus or minus or a *T* or *F* with fingers to answer true-false questions. Students can hold up 1, 2, 3, or 4 fingers to answer multiple-choice questions. Students can nod their heads *yes* or *no* to indicate agreement and disagreement. All of these are informal techniques for diagnoses that give teachers immediate information without the inevitable delay and drudgery of correcting papers. If plagiarism is suspected, saying "Close your eyes and show me" easily identifies those who know and those who need to "take a little peek."

     If the learning is a performance behavior (such as ones in art, music, writing, athletics, drama, dance), observing while students are "doing it" will give the needed diagnostic information.

     A written response of a word, a brief phrase, or a short sentence can provide *sampling* evidence to the circulating teacher. "Jot down a one-sentence summary of the importance of _____, definition of _____, reasons for _____" gives informal diagnostic information as the teacher checks samples of fast, slow, or average students. From the samples, a teacher usually can generalize to the rest of the students in that same category and then make the decision to move on, give more practice, or to go back and reteach.

Inferential Diagnosis

An inference is a judgment about the present based on past experience. An experienced teacher can extrapolate from the performance of similar students in past classes, from this group's past performance, or from a particular student's previous work to make predictions of or assumptions about performance of similar students in the present situation, thereby saving diagnostic time and effort. The prediction constantly needs to be monitored and corrected by continuing informal diagnosis.

No one type of diagnosis is best in all situations. All diagnoses need to be corrected and updated *during* instruction so that teaching decisions are always based on current data. Mountains of paper evidence do not guarantee accuracy; in fact, the information may become obsolete and interfere with working from *current* assessment information.

Monitoring and Adjusting While Teaching

Signaled Responses

To avoid moving on to new material without ascertaining that the student understands or can do the present task, a teacher typically asks questions that require oral or written answers. Oral responses tap only the learning of the particular students who get a chance to respond. The learning of the remainder of the class remains unknown. Written responses from the whole class take time to correct. At times, both of the above procedures are necessary. Much of the time, however, signaled responses accomplish the dual purpose of requiring every student to determine a response and of providing evidence of what each student knows. While it is not always possible to see each student's signal, deviance usually stands out and is easily detected. Also teachers quickly learn at whom to look. As previously explained, creative teachers can design signaled, representational responses for most questions (or opinions if there is no one right answer). They can list and number alternative answers on the board (or in the book) and then have students select one and show the number of the correct answer with their fingers. If appropriate, the teacher can call on students to give the rationale that supports their correct answers so that the others know why they were right or, if they were wrong, how to correct their errors.

Oral Responses

The direction "Say the answer to yourself, but not out loud—just pretend you are talking" should proceed or follow most questions. This activity should occupy "wait time" of a few seconds. Such subvocalizing encourages each student in the group to formulate an answer. It also gives learning the assist by having each student formulate and "hear" the answer in addition to "feeling" subvocal speech. The student, and only the student, knows whether s/he can answer the question. Consequently, lack of knowing is revealed only to the person most in need of that information. Validation or correction occurs when, subsequently, the answer is given out loud by one student or the teacher. "If you said divide, you were correct. Be ready to explain why this problem requires division."

Choral responses after "wait time" can be judged on their strength and unanimity; however, "coattailing" (echoing another student's response) can conceal lack of knowledge. Choral responses are better for initial learning and beginning practice than they are for validating learning.

Observing students as they conduct their own learning is often a better diagnosis than paper and pencil. It also enables teachers to give specific, growth-evoking feedback.

After adequate teaching, the direction "Tell your neighbor" gives each student the opportunity to make an oral response with high probability that the neighbor will build in correction if there is inaccuracy. By circulating, the teacher can sample responses and make diagnostic judgments on the basis of the stratum of the class (more able, less able) that each sampled student represents.

"Say the answer with your lips but not with your voice" makes one-word answers easily read by the teacher.

The oral response is of particular importance to future writing performance. "Construct and say your introductory sentence to yourself. Jot it down if you think you might forget it before you're called on" causes a student to refine his/her own sentence before the class hears it. This technique also gives classmates the opportunity to hear a variety of introductory sentences. As a result, the quality of the sentence eventually written by each student is likely to improve. The problem of effective writing is not so much in encoding script but in conceptualizing, organizing, and polishing the sentences to be written. Teachers of writing who have used this technique of "saying and hearing" in preparation for writing have reported that they have dramatically fewer papers to correct and those papers are of remarkably better quality. Students' thoughtful analysis of others' ideas and their helpful suggestions (not criticism!) accelerate everyone's learning.

Independent Practice After Teaching

Student-Involving Practice

A teacher creating practice pages, then standing over a smoking photocopy machine to duplicate them, is not necessarily contributing the most to students' thinking or learning. Instead, teachers can give simple oral directions for practice that actively engages students in higher-level thinking. Also, letting students create their individual practice often results in more learning by the student. (Of course, students must be shown and taught how to do this, and the teacher should establish the criteria for the practice.) Here are some examples of oral directions for practice that involves the students actively:

1. "List five to ten words in your reader that you could touch (*boy, ball*) and five to ten words you couldn't" (*in, when*) or "List abstract concepts ('courage') and concrete concepts ('round')."
2. "List five ways the main character is like you and five ways s/he is different."
3. "Make up two three-place subtraction problems where you regroup from the tens to the ones, two where you regroup from

the hundreds to the tens, two where you regroup from the hundreds to the ones, and two where you don't regroup."

4. "Using the *same* facts in a story problem, write a question that would require you to add to find the answer, a question requiring subtraction, another question for multiplication, and another for division."

5. "Make up five questions that would test whether someone really understood the chapter. Make sure the answers cannot be found in any one sentence. Star the question you think is best."

A creative teacher can think of endless possibilities that require only verbal directions to the student, yet generate excellent practice that requires high-level thinking. "Star the one you think is best" requires evaluation by the student and enables a teacher who is pressed for time to examine only one response from each student, but additional ones are available if needed for verification of achievement.

Student-Corrected Practice

After students have done a teacher-assigned follow-up or created one of their own, the work can be checked by that student using an answer key, or it can be checked by another student and then returned to the originator to defend or correct. (Remember these are skills and criteria that must be taught and then practiced by students before they can be performed independently.) In peer correction, both the originator and the corrector can learn from the process. Eventually, most papers go the teacher who spot-checks or examines specific students' work.

This process of students' examining other students' work is especially beneficial in learning writing, rewriting, and editing skills. It is not a wise use of time for a teacher to be constantly correcting initial drafts. Students should be *taught* how to edit, rewrite, and polish before submitting a final paper. This process when well-taught will also produce students who can suggest ideas to others without being critical and demeaning, who can take suggestions without being defensive, and who learn that excellence in writing results from working to achieve it.

Homework

Countless wasted hours result from using schooltime to correct daily homework. Homework is assigned so that students develop facility with information, skills, processes, or appreciations after they have been *taught* the necessary skills to do so. The important question to be answered after homework is, "Has the student learned what was intended?," not "Has the student done the homework?" With homework, the teacher never knows *who* has done it; was it the student's parents, brother, sister, friend?

A quick checkup test with one or two of the kinds of problems assigned or one or two sample questions from those asked in the homework will quickly reveal whether the student has *learned*. Certainly, the one question the student does or doesn't remember may not be a fair evaluation of any one assignment, but over time, it will separate those who have learned from those who simply "got it done."

If the student has learned how to do the work (the reason we assign homework, isn't it?), does it matter whether or not s/he "did it"? Somehow we seem to have forgotten the purpose of homework, and we reward doing rather than learning. A quick quiz on homework can be collected and graded by the teacher on some days, while on other days, the answers can be given to students so they can evaluate their own learning. Students won't know which will occur on any one day and so are stimulated to do their best. Also, they will view homework as a help in learning, not a chore to be done.

Conclusion

An important precursor to the use of all of these techniques, which aim at eliminating so much correction of papers, is that the principal and teacher acquaint parents with the important reasons for using such techniques and their resultant, accelerating effect on students' learning. Otherwise, these strategies may be viewed by parents, for whom they are new, as teachers' getting out of work rather than as ways to stimulate students' higher-level thinking, facilitate their learning, and increase their responsibility for learning.

Some teachers also may need to deal with their feelings of guilt for changing "working harder" to "working smarter." Increased learning and independence of students should present convincing evidence that it is better to inspire students than it is to perspire over paperwork.

22

Homework: Asset to Learning or Waste of Time?

Homework is not "good" in and of itself. The value of homework is directly related to the value of what is being learned, as perceived by the student, as well as to the fit of the homework to the objective it was designed to accomplish and to the particular student for whom that objective is appropriate.

Here are some desirable goals that homework can accomplish:

1. Giving practice needed to develop fluency (automaticity) in a particular skill so that skill requires less student (brain or neural) energy, thereby freeing up

Homework should extend or automate essential learnings.

    energy for creative problem solving or new learning (reading, number facts, spelling, writing skills, discovery techniques, problem solving, conversation in a foreign language)

2. Extending or enriching learning beyond that which was taught and accomplished in class (writing questions about a subject; a different ending for a story; creating a poem, picture, puzzle, story; researching an interest)

3. Providing an activity not possible in the classroom (making a food product, gathering samples of leaves or rocks, interviewing parents and other people in the community)

4. Saving instructional time in the classroom (finishing a project that the student knows how to do, recopying an original poem for a class book, developing speed and fluency with learning that needs to become automated)

5. Developing perseverance (making oneself finish, working through a hard but achievable task)

6. Developing productive use of leisure time (extending hobbies— art, music, literature, research interests—that have been introduced in class)

7. Keeping students away from TV or out of their parents' hair (occasionally a needed objective but the activity must also accomplish one of the above objectives and not be "busywork")

Each of these will be examined in turn.

1. Giving Practice Needed for a Particular Skill

Practice on a skill is a prescriptive homework assignment. To be a valid use of time, the practice should be needed by *each* student engaged in it. The teacher also must have evidence, based on the student's previous performance, that the practice is going to be done reasonably correctly; otherwise, homework errors become deeply entrenched and difficult to eradicate. It is seldom that the same *prescriptive* assignment can be given to an entire class unless wide variance in ability can be accommodated: writing a story, drawing a picture. While all students may do homework in one content area (math, spelling, reading, writing), the specific skills they are practicing should differ according to students' needs.

Examples
For particular students, the teacher assigns practice of unlearned number facts, certain spelling words, writing practice. The teacher suggests that each of these be practiced briefly several times, spaced apart, not just once during the evening; for example, during several TV commercials in the course of an evening. Finding main ideas, outlining, summarizing or doing *needed* special reading, writing, or math practice pages are effective assignments that require the students to spend longer periods of time.

2. Extending and Enriching Learning

Homework assignments that extend learning into additional areas to enrich current knowledge and skills require that students use *already acquired* skills, yet go beyond their classroom work.

Examples

- "Read a new book that _____."
- "Find out more about _____."
- "Write a story about _____."
- "Design a new way to _____."
- "Make up some problems that _____."
- "Interview your parents to find out _____."

This homework can be checked by the student sharing with a partner or reporting to the class. It occasionally (and unexpectedly)

Perplexing problems stimulate creative solutions which can be worked out independently

can be graded by the teacher. When every homework assignment is graded, students tend to do it for the grade rather than for extending their learning.

3. Providing Activities Not Possible in the Classroom

Learning becomes useful to problem solving, decision making, and creativity when the learning is applied to a new life situation. Consequently, a productive homework assignment is one that causes a student to transfer skills acquired in the classroom to life outside the classroom.

Examples

- "Use the food ads in the newspaper to list purchases for a well-balanced meal that you would enjoy, and then compute the difference in cost between stores."
- "Use the interviewing techniques you've learned in class and talk with your parents to identify the sources of your family traditions."
- "Keep track of money you spend, and then make a bar graph that groups all your expenditures into any four categories that you create."
- "Make a diagram (time line, slide show, mural) that shows _____."

This kind of homework also can be shared with a partner or the class for enrichment. It does not always need to be checked or graded by the teacher, but the students never know when it will be.

4. Saving Time in the Classroom

When a student can do something without teacher guidance, doing the work at home to prepare for tomorrow's lesson will save instructional time in the classroom.

Examples

- Reading the chapter on the events leading up to the Revolutionary War and being ready to discuss the position taken by each side

- Writing the final version of a report after demonstrating the possession of necessary skills
- Reading to get information, to increase fluency, or to enjoy literature
- Doing distributed practice to maintain or increase accuracy, speed, or fluency in an already-learned area

5. Developing Perseverance

Perseverance (making yourself continue when you are tempted to stop) is needed as students progress through school and through life. Also, as assignments become longer and more complex, students must be able to sustain their effort beyond one evening session.

With the exception of an introduction to a new skill, when a total class skill assignment is given, some students may not need to practice. While it may be appropriate, it is not always politic for a student to call that fact to the teacher's (or their future boss's) attention. While teachers should avoid giving students assignments to practice what they already know, students need to develop the ability to make themselves do something that they think they don't really need to practice or to do something that they may consider, correctly or incorrectly, to be unimportant. (Think of your feelings as you work on your tax forms.)

It is inexcusable, however, for a teacher deliberately to assign homework that a student doesn't need to do. Perseverance is better developed with material or skills that need to be learned.

Negative Examples
(We hope *you* don't assign them!)

- Doing another page of the same problems after the student has already demonstrated fluency
- Writing and rewriting every paper for perfect copy
- Doing an excessive amount of the same kind of assignment (30 of the same math operation, 20 of the same kind of grammatical construction)

A general assignment can be adjusted for more able students by increasing its complexity rather than the amount of work assigned. "Make up what you think would be a fair test of understanding the chapter" or "Create some word problems, based on the chapter, that would require multiplication or division." For less able students, the assignment can be shortened if their problem is time needed rather than their lacking the skills required to do the work. In the latter case, the assignment should be changed to one that, with effort, can be accomplished.

6. Developing Productive Use of Leisure Time

With increased mechanization, students will have more leisure time that they need to fill productively. Appropriate homework encourages students to develop activities that are recreational. They will not have the opportunity to do this if all their time is taken up by assigned academic activities. Art activities, drama, creating skits, dance, music, sports, reading, and creative writing are ones that qualify as appropriate homework so that students develop a wide variety of interests and skills.

7. Keeping Students From TV and out of Parents' Hair

Instead of using homework as a time filler, we strongly urge that both school and home introduce students to many arts and hobbies and then provide time for the student to pursue those of his/her choice. This "homework assignment" will develop a skill needed throughout life, that of productive recreation. An excellent homework assignment is "Turn off the TV and engage in an activity that requires something of you and is something that you really enjoy. Be ready, tomorrow, to report what you did."

Homework need not be "easy." It can be stimulating, valuable, and enjoyable, or it can be such a chore or bore that it turns students off to learning and on to the mental chewing gum of TV. However, TV itself can be a profitable homework assignment when it has a purpose. "Watch this program to see (discover, learn, discuss, analyze) how the effect was created (the main ideas were presented, the characters built, how you were persuaded)." When analyzing TV fulfills one of the valid reasons for homework, a student receives double indemnity from watching. Also, encouraging students to practice a skill during commercials fulfills the need for frequent, short, intense practice periods that produce automaticity (and at the same time the homework takes them away from the "silent persuasion").

Conclusion

Homework is neither good nor bad in itself. It is the kind of homework and its productive results that make it a valuable asset to students' learning. Examine homework assignments you give to see if they enhance all kinds of achievement. Then, develop ways so that home assignments become increasingly stimulating and productive. Encourage students to design their own homework and validate its "worthwhileness."

The research in homework is sparse and neither the "for'ers" or "agin'ers" can claim a solid research base unless the type of homework and its learning results are described. Common sense tells us that if we work, with direction, on something with an intent to improve, the probability is that we'll get better. So it is with homework. Teachers can improve their homework assignments and students can enhance their skills, knowledge, and interests with homework.

Along with a more enlightened and productive approach to homework comes administrators' and teachers' responsibility for educating parents to the value of well-designed homework vs. the amount of homework or busywork that turns students off from extending their learning. District policy also should reflect the requirement that homework be learning-inducing and perceivably complementary to excellence in education rather than routine drudgery.

Excellence in education reflects the best of what we know in what we do. Assigning homework is no exception.

Bibliography

Barber, B. (1986). Homework does not belong on the agenda for educational reform. *Educational Leadership, 43*(8), 55–57.

Cooper, H. (1989). *Homework.* Research on Teaching Monograph Series. New York: Longman.

Dick. D. (1980). Experimental study of the effects of required homework review on request upon achievement. ERIC Document Reproduction Service No. ED 194 320.

Goodlad, J. I. (1983). *A place called school: Prospects for the future.* New York: McGraw-Hill.

Gray, R. S., & Allison, D. E. (1971). An experimental study of the relationship of homework to pupil success in computation with fractions. *School Science and Mathematics, 71,* 339–346.

Paschal, R. A., Weinstein, T., & Walberg, H. J. (1984). The effects of homework on learning: A quantitative synthesis. *Journal of Educational Research,* 98–104.

Walberg, H. J., Paschal, R. A., & Weinstein, T. (1985). Homework's powerful effects on learning. *Educational Leadership, 42*(7), 76–79.

23

Testing and Teaching

"Measurement-driven instruction" became the credo of the eighties and "teaching to the test" the resultant alleged mortal sin. At the same time, accountability had reared its accusing head to denounce the escalating costs of education without accompanying increases in efficiency and effectiveness. As other services have increased in cost (medicine, transportation, computerized offices), we have seen a resultant increase in the quality and/or quantity of their services or products. The public would have us believe this is not so in education, and that, in fact, our services and products have declined.

As a person who is deeply involved in the grass roots of American schooling as well as in research, I would argue that the public is uninformed. Educators know more about what they're doing and how to do it than has been known since the beginning of time. (Other countries are adopting what we have learned, and we are gaining knowledge from them.) Nevertheless, there still exists a major gap between what we know about how the human brain functions in the relationship of teaching to learning and what is occurring in many American classrooms. In this writer's opinion, based on educational work and observation throughout the world, there is an even greater gap between research and practice in most other countries, although students and conditions are markedly different from ours.

Two forces in American education are directed toward closing that gap. One is the surge, now become a tidal wave, of professional development. Educators have accepted the assertion that a professional never ceases learning better ways of delivering services to the client. As a result, staff development is becoming a routine item in any defensible school budget. Rather than lying fallow, entombed in psychological jar-

Important information, processes, and procedures should be taught, then tested.

gon and buried in seldom-read journals, cause-effect relationships between teaching and learning are being translated into language and actions comprehensible to educators, and subsequently those relationships are becoming professionally expressed in daily practice.

The second impetus to narrowing the gap between theory and practice is the national fixation on measurement and accountability. It is to our current focus on testing and teaching that this chapter will be directed.

Some Background on Tests

All educators have been required to take a course in Tests and Measurement and/or Educational Statistics. Most "groaned" through the history of tests beginning with Binet and the Army Alpha, increased their "groans" with "measures of central tendency" and "standard deviations" without having "grown" in their ability to measure results from their own teaching.

Until the last two decades, *norm-referenced* tests were the only ones routinely in the repertoire of school measurement. Such tests are useful in identifying learners in relation to the norming group. For selection purposes, norm-referenced tests identify the best, worst, and those in the average range. Norm-referenced tests permit the comparison of groups in School X to those in School Y, even though the composition of those groups may be very different. Unfortunately, norm-referenced tests (standardized achievement tests) are frequently used to make judgments for which they were not designed.

Criterion-referenced tests measure each individual in relation to a specified performance criterion. Can the learner write a persuasive essay, use specified punctuation marks correctly, add with regrouping, factor quadratics, state the issues involved in the Civil War? A criterion-referenced test answers the measurement question with "Yes, s/he can" or "No, s/he can't." It is a certification that students have or have not learned a specified content or process regardless of whether other students have learned more or less.

As a result, criterion-referenced testing is increasingly becoming one "driver" of instruction. Well-designed, criterion tests have become a major propellant in successful curriculum design and instruction. Poorly conceived and constructed, criterion tests become an endless list of trivialized pieces of information that are easily measured but that contribute little of significance to the important cognitive, affective, or psychomotor outcomes required of today's schooling.

More recently, student "portfolios" have come into prominence as "time-elapse indicators" of student progress. Portfolios of products that sup-

Portraying a story through actions is an excellent test of understanding.
Polishing that performance for an audience builds rigor.

ply visual and/or auditory evidence of achievement have always been sub-
mitted by people who were judged by what they could produce: artists,
architects, inventors, dancers, musicians, writers, actors, and editors.

Students now are being asked to design, compose, and submit tan-
gible evidence of more complex processes and achievements (writing,
designing, experimenting, visual or auditory products) because these
achievements cannot be measured, easily and accurately, by short paper-
and-pencil tests.

Evaluation of a student no longer needs to be based only on a one-
time measurement, but can be augmented by objective evidence of how
much growth has occurred over a period of time. Time-sample evidence
is an important predictor of the growth expected in the future.

As an obvious example, suppose Jumper A can clear a 4-foot bar,
while Jumper B can clear only a 2-foot bar. Both jumpers have the same
period of coaching from the same coach. Subsequently, Jumper A still can
clear only 4 feet. Jumper B can clear 3 feet, 10 inches. Who do you predict will jump higher in the future?

Thus, portfolios not only give objective evidence of accomplishment but have predictive value. The major question now is, "What should the contents of the portfolio be to validate growth in a specified area?" Bushel baskets of what students have done will not serve the purpose. Student and teacher together need to determine what should be included to provide the most valid evidence of accomplishment, yet be economical in terms of time required of both teacher and student. This selection of evidence is one of the most important questions to be addressed as we develop this time-based assessment of student achievement. We are only at the beginning of answering it.

Teacher-Developed Testing

We need measurement experts to design the high-stakes tests that become major determinants of a student's future. The typical classroom teacher or school administrator has neither the time nor the training to perform the arduous task of developing valid and reliable achievement tests. Teachers, however, need to be able to create their own valid tests of what their students have or have not learned. Teachers use more information from these daily assessments than they do from most commercial standardized tests. Yet teachers have little training or experience in valid test construction or in analytic interpretations of the results. Both skills—test construction and test interpretation—are essential to excellence in instruction. How to construct informal but valid criterion tests and portfolios needs to become a major, long overdue objective in teacher preparation and in staff development programs.

Currently, at the end of a unit, a tired teacher sits down the night before the administration of a test and wonders, "What questions should I ask on a test so I can give students their grades?" Consideration of that important question "What will be tested at the end of the unit?" needs to occur *before* the instruction for that unit is designed. What are the important outcomes that should result from this episode of instruction, and how will those outcomes be validated and measured? The answers to those questions become the basis of instructional planning and the criteria of students' successful achievement.

Creating the final outcome before planning the unit does not limit what will be learned; much more can be added if there is time or if a better outcome emerges. It is a clear focus, not constraint, that is added to the learning opportunity. Students will be evaluated on something they, for sure, have had the opportunity to learn rather than what is "hoped" will be achieved. Also, it alerts teachers to check, *while teaching*, that students are growing in the essential skills rather than moving on without essential learnings having been accomplished, only to discover this discrepancy at the end of the instructional period.

An unfortunate occurrence that is even more pervasive is the daily lesson that "covers" material with little or no understanding of what is to be accomplished and why, and no evidence that it has been accomplished before moving on.

Regardless of whether the final outcome has been determined as "The learner will solve equations requiring factoring of quadratics" or "The learner will write a persuasive essay on a subject of his/her choice" or "The learner will develop potential solutions to a class problem" or "The learner will compare the Alps to the Andes," articulating these outcome behaviors helps the teacher determine the best mode for delivering instruction: whether cooperative learning, discovery, computer-assisted instruction, direct teaching, or any other model would result in the greatest probability of yielding successful achievement.

Having answered the "end of the instructional period" question, the teacher should ask the next planning question, "What knowledge or skills, essential to that outcome, do these students already possess?" This baseline may be inferred or it can be measured by a formal test or informal observation. (See chapter 5.)

As instruction occurs, informal testing, observation, sampled answers, or signaled answers from students frequently give a teacher reasonably accurate information that can constantly be verified or corrected. Signaled answers, in which, for example, students use hand signals such as making a *T* or *F* to show true or false, were as major a breakthrough in education as was penicillin in medicine. Now we can "cure" lack of knowledge, uncertainty, or confusion, even for complex content, right when these occur rather than wait for a final test to reveal them long after the optimal point for remediation.

The observations and signaled and/or sampled responses often can be used to ascertain reasonably accurate baseline data and to measure the success of daily instruction informally *only if* the teacher knows what needs to be measured and how to design questions that will economically and accurately assess that information and/or process. "With your fingers on one hand make the two dots of a colon or make the dot and comma of a semicolon with two hands. Which does this sentence require?" will give either baseline or "en route" information during colon or semicolon instruction. If plagiarism is a problem, the direction "Close your eyes and signal" will reveal those who are not answering on their own.

"See how many of the five causes (factors, principles, elements) you can list. Say them to yourself and put up one finger for each one you remember and are ready to explain" will give informal information as to whether a teacher needs to review or reteach. Calling first on students who have the least number of fingers up gives them a chance to contribute and challenges more able students to subtract what they hear from what they remember for their subsequent contribution. In this way, all students have had feedback on what they know and what they need to learn. They have "taken a test" and had it corrected without the discouraging effects of a poor grade. Those who need it have the warning that they are not yet prepared for the graded evaluation. Many such informal assessments contribute to students' knowledge of their own progress before the criterion test.

Informally testing progress or creating portfolios during instruction prepares students for predictable success on the evaluations at the end of instruction *if* the learning opportunities are well designed to accomplish the intended outcome and *if* the evaluation instruments were constructed to economically and accurately measure what was to be learned.

Let's look at how measurement-driven instruction can function with both a simple and a complex objective, using the most economical and discerning criterion test.

Examples
Here is an example of a simple math objective.

Instructional Objective: The learner will make change from a dollar for a purchase of less than a dollar, using the fewest number of coins without half-dollars.

Criterion Test: The learner will make change for a 7-cent purchase. (This requires the use of every coin.) If a student can do this example correctly, there is high probability that all other possibilities also can be done correctly.

Here is an example of a more complex language arts objective.

Instructional Objective: The learner will write a persuasive argument on a known subject.

Criterion Test: On the subject of less homework, the learner will make explicit, and support with data, his/her point of view, anticipate teacher's and parents' counterarguments, then dilute or refute those arguments, and present all of the above in a well-designed, cogent, and technically correct piece of writing.

Each of these criterion tests can be included in a portfolio to show students' achievement. Each makes explicit what needs to be learned so "teaching to the test" involves teaching the information or skills that will generalize to a successful response. This is *not* teaching the answer to a specific test question.

Testing and teaching are not adversarial; each contributes to the accomplishment of the other. To realize the major educational dividends from their productive relationship, we need to redesign teacher and administrative preparation and inservice training so today's educational professionals are well equipped to interpret and correctly utilize results from norm-referenced and criterion-referenced, high-stakes tests designed by experts, or from portfolios designed by teacher and student. Even more important is the teacher's ability to construct valid informal daily and end-of-unit tests so that measurement-driven instruction plus excellence in varied instructional procedures produces outcomes of increasing quality and quantity in American education.

Bibliography

Airasian, P. W. (1991). *Classroom assessment.* New York: McGraw-Hill.

Crooks, T. J. (1988). The impact of classroom evaluation practices on students. *Review of Educational Research, 58*(34), 438–481.

Ennis, R. H. (1985). A logical base for measuring critical thinking skills. *Educational Leadership, 43*(2), 44–48.

Greenlund, N. (1985). *Measurement and evaluation in teaching* (5th ed.). New York: Macmillan.

Gronlund, N. E. (1992). *How to make achievement tests and assessments* (5th ed.). Boston: Allyn & Bacon.

Harmon, J. L., Aschbacher, P., & Winters, L. (1992). *A practical guide to alternative assessment.* Alexandria, VA: Association for Supervision and Curriculum Development.

Henman, Joan. (1992). What research tells us about good assessment. *Educational Leadership, 49*(8), 74–79.

Popham, J. (1990). *Modern educational measurement: A practitioner's perspective.* Englewood Cliffs, NJ: Prentice-Hall.

Popham, J. (1993). *Educational evaluation* (3rd ed.). Boston: Allyn & Bacon.

Wittrock, M. C., & Baker, E. (1991). *Testing and cognition.* Englewood Cliffs, NJ: Prentice-Hall.

24

Education: The Ultimate Profession

Education and medicine are parallel professions. Both are dedicated to the welfare of humankind. Both work where no certainty exists, only high probability. (People die who shouldn't; people live when all indications are that they won't. Some students learn or don't learn in spite of what might be predicted.)

Both professions began with intuition, folklore, experience, and fantasy that later was subjected to rigorous examination to develop cause and most probable effects. Both professions continue to add skills with highly probable outcomes as research makes discoveries. Both are applied sciences. Medicine works from knowledge of

Helping students learn to find answers to their own questions builds life-long competence and confidence.

chemistry and physics, education from knowledge of psychology and sociology.

Both professions began with pathology: medicine with curing the sick, education with remedial programs for students who hadn't learned. Now, the focus of each is on prevention rather than remediation. The major thrust of current medical practice is on promoting and maintaining health, although it still cures the sick. As a result, illness is being reduced.

The major thrust of education is on promoting and maintaining learning so that "all students will learn" with whatever professional assistance is necessary to ensure their success.

Education and medicine also are different. Medicine has been adding to its store of knowledge and practice for thousands of years, starting with "what works" and then testing that experiential knowledge in laboratory settings. Psychology, the science of human learning and behavior that is the basis of education, is only a century old. Sociology, as it pertains to groups of learners, is an even more recent science. So it is only relatively recently that experience in teaching has begun to be substantiated or challenged by the strict standards of scientific examination.

Teaching and surgery are similar in that a professional prepares a plan of action that subsequently must be modified "on the spot" as a result of continuously emerging data. Surgeons can't admonish the patient to "Stop bleeding until I get this done!" They must immediately adjust their actions on the basis of unanticipated reactions of the patient. Teachers can't admonish the fire alarm to stop or Susie not to get sick "until we finish this problem."

Although surgeons have life and death in their hands at any one second, they have only one patient who is sedated and holding still. They do not have to monitor others in the hospital to see that they are not tearing up the sheets or pouring out the medicine.

Teachers affect eternity.

Teachers do not have life and death in their hands at any one moment, but they do affect the enhancement or death of student self-esteem, success, and zest for learning. Most kindergarten students come to school eager to learn: "Here I am you lucky world!" By the third grade, some of them are "turned off," feeling they are no good, unliked, or dumb. Most homes don't send them that way; it happens, inadvertently, *not* intentionally, at school.

Teachers, also, must constantly adjust their plans as a result of students' responses and nonverbal behaviors. Teachers have multiple "patients" to monitor while working with a large group, a small group, or an individual. Theirs is an equally demanding, highly scientific profession where art and intuition exist to complement science, as they do in medicine.

Most students begin school with delight in learning and with each other.

Education is our most important profession. The future of this world, in fact, depends on its educators. It is they who are producing the diplomats who eventually will negotiate world peace and the citizens who will not perceive diversity as deficiency. Of course, parents "born" students and are a powerful influence in their early years, but students will learn diplomatic skills, international policies, and a respect for diversity in schools that are focused on these outcomes.

In like manner, educators are producing the scientists and physicians who eventually will cure currently incurable diseases. Chemistry, physics, anatomy, and physiology are learned in schools. The environmentalists who will restore our world to a healthy, productive place that accommodates humans, plants, and animals are learning their essential skills in schools. The business and service people who keep our world running effectively, the architects and engineers who make our world beautiful and functional, and the artists of music, dance, drama, and the visual arts, no matter what their generic talent and family support—all are the results of educational experiences and direction.

Future students who come to school eager and ready to learn usually come from parents who had a productive experience in their own schooling and have transmitted that expectation to their children. Again, excellent teachers are the major cause.

So practice your profession with pride, with research-based knowledge and skills that you translate into daily artistic practice, and with a real commitment to continually enhancing your skills so that you expertly contribute to your students' emotional, social, physical, and academic well-being. The world can be a better place because you are a teacher. The impact of your influence will never end.

Bibliography

Kysilka, M. (1990). *Honor in teaching: Reflections*. West Lafayette, IN: Kappa Delta Pi Publications.

Index

Factor analysis, 8
Feedback, 14
Film, of teaching techniques, 9, 13
"Fogging," 208
Formal diagnosis, 215
Freud, Sigmund, 21

Gage, Nate, 23
Generalizations
defined, 66, 67
on teaching, 73–74
teaching of, 70
Generative theory of learning,
168–169
Genetic predispositions, 118–121
Group choral response, 92, 217
Guided/monitored practice, 92–93

Handbook of Research on Teaching
(Gage), 23
Hemispheres of brain. *See* Brain
hemispheres
Homework, 219–220, 221–228
extending and enriching learning
through, 224–225
goals of, 221–223
for particular skill, 223
perseverance and, 226–227
as productive use of leisure time,
227
saving classroom time with,
225–226
television and, 227
Hunter model of teaching, 29–46
elements of, 42–44
myths and misunderstandings
about, 31–35
problems with use of, 35–37, 38
research on, 34–35

Imaging, 110, 125, 126
Imitation. *See* Modeling
Independent practice, 218–220
homework, 219–220, 221–228
lesson design and, 93–94
student-corrected, 219
student-involving, 218–219

time for, 163–165
Independent sequence, 79
Inferential diagnosis, 216
Informal diagnosis, 215–216
Information
elaborative rehearsal of, 109–112
judging authenticity of, 182
organization of, 112–113
rote rehearsal of, 108–109
visual-spatial, 123–124, 128, 132
Input. *See* Instructional input
Instructional elements, 35, 45
Instructional input
lesson design and, 89–90
right-brained vs. left-brained,
121–124
source and type of, 3
Instructional objectives, 3, 77–84
anticipatory set and, 95
attributes of, 52
cautions about, 80–84
student awareness of, 94–95
understanding, 78–80
Instructional time, 156, 158–163
Interest, arousal of, 104–108
IQ, 21, 119–120
ITIP. *See* Hunter model of teaching

Key words, 133–134
Knowledge
conditional, 30, 36, 43–44
procedural, 30, 43–44
propositional, 30, 43–44

Labeling, 90
Learning. *See also* Observational
learning
cooperative, 207
extending and enriching through
homework, 224–225
generative theory of, 168–169
repetition of answers and,
203–205
research on, 26–27
transfer through examples,
168–169
Learning behaviors, 11–12, 99–101

Madeline Hunter

Madeline Hunter left a 20-year assignment as principal of the lab school and professor at UCLA to become a full-time professor in administration and teacher education there, as well as an international consultant. She is the author of 13 books and more than 300 journal articles that translate psychological theory into educational practice. Her programs to increase teaching effectiveness and to develop principals and supervisors as educational/instructional leaders are used in every state and on all continents. She is a continuing consultant to the U.S. Department of Defense, U.S.Department of State, and many industries.

Dr. Hunter began her career as a clinical psychologist in the Los Angeles Children's Hospital and then moved to Juvenile Hall. In both of these positions, she felt she was delivering "too little, too late," so she changed to the preventive orientation of a school psychologist. In that position, she found that educators had little knowledge of cause-effect relationships between teaching and learning, so she began conducting inservice classes to translate psychological theory into classroom practice. Dr. Hunter has held all positions up to assistant superintendent in the public schools of California.

Dr. Hunter has received many awards: recently, the Chief State School Officers Award for Contribution to Education in the 50 States, the Distinguished Professor Award from the American Association of School Administrators, and the Distinguished Service to Education Award from the National Elementary Principals Association. She has been made a Kentucky Colonel, an Arkansas Traveler, and an honorary citizen of Texas. Recently, she was named as one of the hundred most influential women of the century and one of the ten most influential in education.